THE BRIDE OF MESSINA

FRIEDRICH SCHILLER

THE BRIDE OF MESSINA DRAMATIS PERSONAE.

ISABELLA, Princess of Messina. DON MANUEL | her Sons. DON CAESAR | BEATRICE. DIEGO, an ancient Servant. MESSENGERS. THE ELDERS OF MESSINA, mute. THE CHORUS, consisting of the Followers of the two Princes.

SCENE I.

A spacious hall, supported on columns, with entrances on both sides; at the back of the stage a large folding-door leading to a chapel.

DONNA ISABELLA in mourning; the ELDERS OF MESSINA.

ISABELLA. Forth from my silent chamber's deep recesses, Gray Fathers of the State, unwillingly I come; and, shrinking from your gaze, uplift The veil that shades my widowed brows: the light And glory of my days is fled forever! And best in solitude and kindred gloom To hide these sable weeds, this grief-worn frame, Beseems the mourner's heart. A mighty voice Inexorable--duty's stern command, Calls me to light again. Not twice the moon Has filled her orb since to the tomb ye bore My princely spouse, your city's lord, whose arm Against a world of envious foes around Hurled fierce defiance! Still his spirit lives In his heroic sons, their country's pride: Ye marked how sweetly from their childhood's bloom They grew in joyous promise to the years Of manhood's strength; yet in their secret hearts, From some mysterious root accursed, upsprung Unmitigable, deadly hate, that spurned All kindred ties, all youthful, fond affections, Still ripening with their thoughtful age; not mine The sweet accord of family bliss; though each Awoke a mother's rapture; each alike Smiled at my nourishing breast! for me alone Yet lives one mutual thought, of children's love; In these tempestuous souls discovered else By mortal strife and thirst of fierce revenge.

While yet their father reigned, his stern control Tamed their hot spirits, and with iron yoke To awful justice bowed their stubborn will: Obedient to his voice, to outward seeming They calmed their wrathful mood, nor in array Ere met, of hostile arms; yet unappeased Sat brooding malice in their bosoms' depths; They little reek of hidden springs whose power Can quell the torrent's fury: scarce their sire In death had closed his eyes, when, as the spark That long in smouldering embers sullen lay, Shoots forth a towering flame; so unconfined Burst the wild storm of brothers' hate triumphant O'er nature's holiest bands. Ye saw, my friends, Your country's bleeding wounds, when princely strife Woke discord's maddening fires, and ranged her sons In mutual deadly conflict;

all around Was heard the clash of arms, the din of carnage, And e'en these halls were stained with kindred gore.

Torn was the state with civil rage, this heart With pangs that mothers feel; alas, unmindful Of aught but public woes, and pitiless You sought my widow's chamber--there with taunts And fierce reproaches for your country's ills From that polluted spring of brother's hate Derived, invoked a parent's warning voice, And threatening told of people's discontent And princes' crimes! "Ill-fated land! now wasted By thy unnatural sons, ere long the prey Of foeman's sword! Oh, haste," you cried, "and end This strife! bring peace again, or soon Messina Shall bow to other lords." Your stern decree Prevailed; this heart, with all a mother's anguish O'erlabored, owned the weight of public cares. I flew, and at my children's feet, distracted, A suppliant lay; till to my prayers and tears The voice of nature answered in their breasts!

Here in the palace of their sires, unarmed, In peaceful guise Messina shall behold The long inveterate foes; this is the day! E'en now I wait the messenger that brings The tidings of my sons' approach: be ready To give your princes joyful welcome home With reverence such as vassals may beseem. Bethink ye to fulfil your subject duties, And leave to better wisdom weightier cares. Dire was their strife to them, and to the State Fruitful of ills; yet, in this happy bond Of peace united, know that they are mighty To stand against a world in arms, nor less Enforce their sovereign will against yourselves.

[The ELDERS retire in silence; she beckons to an old attendant, who remains.

Diego!

DIEGO. Honored mistress!

ISABELLA. Old faithful servant, then true heart, cone near me; Sharer of all a mother's woes, be thine The sweet communion of her joys: my treasure Shrined in thy heart, my dear and holy secret Shall pierce the envious veil, and shine triumphant To cheerful day; too long by harsh decrees, Silent and overpowered, affection yet Shall utterance find in Nature's tones of rapture! And this imprisoned heart leap to the embrace Of all it holds most dear, returned to glad My desolate halls; So bend thy aged steps To the old cloistered sanctuary that guards The darling of my soul, whose innocence To thy true love (sweet pledge of happier days)! Trusting I gave, and asked from fortune's storm A resting place and shrine. Oh, in this hour Of bliss; the dear reward of all thy cares. Give to my longing arms my child again! [Trumpets are heard in the distance.

Haste! be thy footsteps winged with joy--I hear The trumpet's blast, that tells in warlike accents My sons are near:

[Exit DIEGO. Music is heard in an opposite direction, and becomes gradually louder.

Messina is awake! Hark! how the stream of tongues hoarse murmuring Rolls on the breeze,--'tis they! my mother's heart Feels their approach, and beats with mighty throes Responsive to the loud, resounding march! They come! they come! my children! oh, my children!

[Exit.

The CHORUS enters.

(It consists of two semi-choruses which enter at the same time from opposite sides, and after marching round the stage range themselves in rows, each on the side by which it entered. One semi-chorus consists of young knights, the other of older ones, each has its peculiar costume and ensigns. When the two choruses stand opposite to each other, the march ceases, and the two leaders speak.) [The first chorus consists of Cajetan, Berengar, Manfred, Tristan, and eight followers of Don Manuel. The second of Bohemund, Roger, Hippolyte, and nine others of the party of Don Caesar.

First Chorus (CAJETAN).

I greet ye, glittering halls Of olden time Cradle of kings! Hail! lordly roof, In pillared majesty sublime!

Sheathed be the sword! In chains before the portal lies The fiend with tresses snake-entwined, Fell Discord! Gently treat the inviolate floor! Peace to this royal dome! Thus by the Furies' brood we swore, And all the dark, avenging Deities! Second Chorus (BOHEMUND).

I rage! I burn! and scarce refrain To lift the glittering steel on high, For, lo! the Gorgon-visaged train Of the detested foeman nigh:

Shall I my swelling heart control? To parley deign--or still in mortal strife The tumult of my soul? Dire sister, guardian of the spot, to thee Awestruck I bend the knee, Nor dare with arms profane thy deep tranquillity!

First Chorus (CAJETAN).

Welcome the peaceful strain! Together we adore the guardian power Of these august abodes! Sacred the hour To kindred brotherly ties And reverend, holy sympathies;-- Our hearts the genial charm shall own, And melt awhile at friendship's soothing tone:-- But when in yonder plain We meet--then peace away! Come gleaming arms, and battle's deadly fray!

The whole Chorus.

But when in yonder plain We meet--then peace away! Come gleaming arms, and battle's deadly fray!

First Chorus (BERENGAR).

I hate thee not--nor call thee foe, My brother! this our native earth, The land that gave our fathers birth:-- Of chief's behest the slave decreed, The vassal draws the sword at need, For chieftain's rage we strike the blow, For stranger lords our kindred blood must flow.

Second Chorus (BOHEMUND).

Hate fires their souls--we ask not why;-- At honor's call to fight and die, Boast of the true and brave! Unworthy of a soldier's name Who burns not for his chieftain's fame!

The whole Chorus. Unworthy of a soldier's name Who burns not for his chieftain's fame! One of the Chorus (BERENGAR).

Thus spoke within my bosom's core The thought--as hitherward I strayed; And pensive 'mid the waving store, I mused, of autumn's yellow glade:-- These gifts of nature's bounteous reign,-- The teeming earth, and golden grain, Yon elms, among whose leaves entwine The tendrils of the clustering vine;-- Gay children of our sunny clime,-- Region of spring's eternal prime! Each charm should woo to love and joy, No cares the dream of bliss annoy, And pleasure through life's summer day Speed every laughing hour away.

We rage in blood,--oh, dire disgrace! For this usurping, alien race; From some far distant land they came, Beyond the sun's departing flame. And owned upon our friendly shore The welcome of our sires of yore. Alas! their sons in thraldom pine, The vassals of this stranger line.

A second (MANFRED).

Yes! pleased, on our land, from his azure way, The sun ever smiles with unclouded ray. But never, fair isle, shall thy sons repose 'Mid the sweets which the faithless waves enclose. On their bosom they wafted the corsair bold, With his dreaded barks to our coast of old. For thee was thy dower of beauty vain, 'Twas the treasure that lured the spoiler's train. Oh, ne'er from these smiling vales shall rise A sword for our vanquished liberties; 'Tis not where the laughing Ceres reigns, And the jocund lord of the flowery plains:-- Where the iron lies hid in the mountain cave, Is the cradle of empire--the home of the brave!

[The folding-doors at the back of the stage are thrown open. DONNA ISABELLA appears between her sons, DON MANUEL and DON CAESAR.

Both Choruses (CAJETAN).

Lift high the notes of praise! Behold! where lies the awakening sun, She comes, and from her queenly brow Shoots glad, inspiring rays. Mistress, we bend to thee! First Chorus.

Fair is the moon amid the starry choir That twinkle o'er the sky, Shining in silvery, mild tranquillity;-- The mother with her sons more fair! See! blooming at her side, She leads the royal, youthful pair; With gentle grace, and soft, maternal pride, Attempering sweet their manly fire.

Second Chorus (BERENGAR).

From this fair stem a beauteous tree With ever-springing boughs shall smile, And with immortal verdure shade our isle; Mother of heroes, joy to thee! Triumphant as the sun thy kingly race Shall spread from clime to clime, And give a deathless name to rolling time!

ISABELLA (comes forward with her SONS). Look down! benignant Queen of Heaven, and still, This proud tumultuous heart, that in my breast Swells with a mother's tide of ecstasy, As blazoned in these noble youths, my image More perfect shows;--Oh, blissful hour! the first That comprehends the fulness of my joy, When long-constrained affection dares to pour In unison of transport from my heart, Unchecked, a parent's undivided love: Oh! it was ever one--my sons were twain. Say--shall I revel in the dreams of bliss, And give my soul to Nature's dear emotions? Is this warm pressure of thy brother's hand A dagger in thy breast? [To DON MANUEL. Or when my eyes Feed on that brow with love's enraptured gaze, Is it a wrong to thee? [To DON CAESAR. Trembling, I pause, Lest e'en affection's breath should wake the fires Of slumbering hate. [After regarding both with inquiring looks Speak! In your secret hearts What purpose dwells? Is it the ancient feud Unreconciled, that in your father's halls A moment stilled; beyond the castle gates, Where sits infuriate war, and champs the bit-- Shall rage anew in mortal, bloody conflict?

Chorus (BOHEMUND). Concord or strife--the fate's decree Is bosomed yet in dark futurity! What comes, we little heed to know, Prepared for aught the hour may show!

ISABELLA (looking round). What mean these arms? this warlike, dread array, That in the palace of your sires portends Some fearful issue? needs a mother's heart Outpoured, this rugged witness of her joys? Say, in these folding arms shall treason hide The deadly snare? Oh, these rude, pitiless men, The ministers of your wrath!--trust not the show Of seeming friendship; treachery in their breasts Lurks to betray, and long-dissembled hate. Ye are a race of other lands; your sires Profaned their soil; and ne'er the invader's yoke Was easy--never in the vassal's heart Languished the hope of sweet revenge;--our sway Not rooted in a people's love, but owns Allegiance from their fears; with secret joy-- For conquest's ruthless sword, and thraldom's chains From age to age, they wait the atoning hour Of princes' downfall;--thus their bards awake The patriot strain, and thus from sire to son Rehearsed, the old traditionary tale Beguiles the winter's night.

False is the world, My sons, and light are all the specious ties By fancy twined: friendship--deceitful name! Its gaudy flowers but deck our summer fortune, To wither at the first rude breath of autumn! So happy to whom heaven has given a brother; The friend by nature signed--the true and steadfast! Nature alone is honest--nature only-- When all we trusted strews the wintry shore-- On her eternal anchor lies at rest, Nor heeds the tempest's rage.

DON MANUEL. My mother! DON CAESAR. Hear me

ISABELLA (taking their hands). Be noble, and forget the fancied wrongs Of boyhood's age: more godlike is forgiveness Than victory, and in your father's grave Should sleep the ancient hate:--Oh, give your days Renewed henceforth to peace and holy love!

[She recedes one or two steps, as if to give them space to approach each other. Both fix their eyes on the ground without regarding one another. ISABELLA (after awaiting for some time, with suppressed emotion, a demonstration on the part of her sons). I can no more; my prayers--my tears are vain:-- 'Tis well! obey the demon in your hearts! Fulfil your dread intent, and stain with blood The holy altars of your household gods;-- These halls that gave you birth, the stage where murder Shall hold his festival of mutual carnage Beneath a mother's eye!--then, foot to foot, Close, like the Theban pair, with maddening gripe, And fold each other in a last embrace! Each press with vengeful thrust the dagger home, And "Victory!" be your shriek of death:--nor then Shall discord rest appeased; the very flame That lights your funeral pyre shall tower dissevered In ruddy columns to the skies, and tell With horrid image--"thus they lived and died!"

[She goes away; the BROTHERS stand as before. Chorus (CAJETAN).

How have her words with soft control Resistless calmed the tempest of my soul! No guilt of kindred blood be mine! Thus with uplifted hands I prey; Think, brothers, on the awful day, And tremble at the wrath divine!

DON CAESAR (without taking his eyes from the ground). Thou art my elder--speak--without dishonor I yield to thee.

DON MANUEL. One gracious word, an instant, My tongue is rival in the strife of love!

DON CAESAR. I am the guiltier--weaker----

DON MANUEL. Say not so! Who doubts thy noble heart, knows thee not well; The words were prouder, if thy soul were mean.

DON CAESAR. It burns indignant at the thought of wrong—But thou--methinks--in passion's fiercest mood, 'Twas aught but scorn that harbored in thy breast. DON MANUEL. Oh! had I known thy spirit thus to peace Inclined, what thousand griefs had never torn A mother's heart!

DON CAESAR. I find thee just and true: Men spoke thee proud of soul.

DON MANUEL. The curse of greatness! Ears ever open to the babbler's tale.

DON CAESAR. Thou art too proud to meanness--I to falsehood! DON MANUEL. We are deceived, betrayed!

DON CAESAR. The sport of frenzy! DON MANUEL. And said my mother true, false is the world?

DON CAESAR. Believe her, false as air. DON MANUEL. Give me thy hand!

DON CAESAR. And thine be ever next my heart!

[They stand clasping each other's hands, and regard each other in silence.

DON MANUEL. I gaze Upon thy brow, and still behold my mother In some dear lineament.

DON CAESAR. Her image looks From thine, and wondrous in my bosom wakes Affection's springs.

DON MANUEL. And is it thou?--that smile Benignant on thy face?--thy lips that charm With gracious sounds of love and dear forgiveness?

DON CAESAR. Is this my brother, this the hated foe? His mien all gentleness and truth, his voice, Whose soft prevailing accents breathe of friendship! [After a pause.

DON MANUEL. Shall aught divide us? DON CAESAR. We are one forever! [They rush into each other's arms.

First CHORUS (to the Second).

Why stand we thus, and coldly gaze, While Nature's holy transports burn? No dear embrace of happier days The pledge--that discord never shall return! Brothers are they by kindred band; We own the ties of home and native land.

[Both CHORUSES embrace. A MESSENGER enters.

Second CHORUS to DON CAESAR (BOHEMUND). Rejoice, my prince, thy messenger returns And mark that beaming smile! the harbinger Of happy tidings.

MESSENGER. Health to me, and health To this delivered state! Oh sight of bliss, That lights mine eyes with rapture! I behold Their hands in sweet accord entwined; the sons Of my departed lord, the princely pair Dissevered late by conflict's hottest rage.

DON CAESAR. Yes, from the flames of hate, a new-born Phoenix, Our love aspires!

MESSENGER. I bring another joy; My staff is green with flourishing shoots.

DON CAESAR (taking him aside). Oh, tell me Thy gladsome message. MESSENGER. All is happiness On this auspicious day; long sought, the lost one Is found.

DON CAESAR. Discovered! Oh, where is she? Speak! MESSENGER. Within Messina's walls she lies concealed.

DON MANUEL (turning to the First SEMI-CHORUS). A ruddy glow mounts in my brother's cheek, And pleasure dances in his sparkling eye; Whate'er the spring, with sympathy of love My inmost heart partakes his joy.

DON CAESAR (to the MESSENGER). Come, lead me; Farewell, Don Manuel; to meet again Enfolded in a mother's arms! I fly To cares of utmost need.

[He is about to depart.

DON MANUEL. Make no delay; And happiness attend thee!

DON CAESAR (after a pause of reflection, he returns). How thy looks Awake my soul to transport! Yes, my brother, We shall be friends indeed! This hour is bright With glad presage of ever-springing love, That in the enlivening beam shall flourish fair, Sweet recompense of wasted years!

DON MANUEL. The blossom Betokens goodly fruit.

DON CAESAR. I tear myself Reluctant from thy arms, but think not less If thus I break this festal hour--my heart Thrills with a holy joy.

DON MANUEL (with manifest absence of mind). Obey the moment! Our lives belong to love.

DON CESAR. What calls me hence----

DON MANUEL. Enough! thou leav'st thy heart. DON CAESAR. No envious secret Shall part us long; soon the last darkening fold Shall vanish from my breast.

[Turning to the CHORUS.

Attend! Forever Stilled is our strife; he is my deadliest foe, Detested as the gates of hell, who dares To blow the fires of discord; none may hope To win my love, that with malicious tales Encroach upon a brother's ear, and point With busy zeal of false, officious friendship. The dart of some rash, angry word, escaped From passion's heat; it wounds not from the lips, But, swallowed by suspicion's greedy ear, Like a rank, poisonous weed, embittered creeps, And hangs about her with a thousand shoots, Perplexing nature's ties.

[He embraces his brother again, and goes away accompanied by the Second CHORUS.

Chorus (CAJETAN). Wondering, my prince, I gaze, for in thy looks some mystery Strange-seeming shows: scarce with abstracted mien And cold thou answered'st, when with earnest heart Thy brother poured the strain of dear affection. As in a dream thou stand'st, and lost in thought, As though--dissevered from its earthly frame-- Thy spirit roved afar. Not thine the breast That deaf to nature's voice, ne'er owned the throbs Of kindred love:--nay more--like one entranced In bliss, thou look'st around, and smiles of rapture Play on thy cheek.

DON MANUEL. How shall my lips declare The transports of my swelling heart? My brother Revels in glad surprise, and from his breast Instinct with strange new-felt emotions, pours The tide of joy; but mine--no hate came with me, Forgot the very spring of mutual strife! High o'er this earthly sphere, on rapture's wings, My spirit floats; and in the azure sea,

Above--beneath--no track of envious night Disturbs the deep serene! I view these halls, And picture to my thoughts the timid joy Of my sweet bride, as through the palace gates, In pride of queenly state, I lead her home. She loved alone the loving one, the stranger, And little deems that on her beauteous brow Messina's prince shall 'twine the nuptial wreath. How sweet, with unexpected pomp of greatness, To glad the darling of my soul! too long I brook this dull delay of crowning bliss! Her beauty's self, that asks no borrowed charm, Shall shine refulgent, like the diamond's blaze That wins new lustre from the circling gold!

Chorus (CAJETAN). Long have I marked thee, prince, with curious eye, Foreboding of some mystery deep enshrined Within thy laboring breast. This day, impatient, Thy lips have burst the seal; and unconstrained Confess a lover's joy;--the gladdening chase, The Olympian coursers, and the falcon's flight Can charm no more:--soon as the sun declines Beneath the ruddy west, thou hiest thee quick To some sequestered path, of mortal eye Unseen--not one of all our faithful train Companion of thy solitary way. Say, why so long concealed the blissful flame? Stranger to fear--ill-brooked thy princely heart One thought unuttered.

DON MANUEL. Ever on the wing Is mortal joy;--with silence best we guard The fickle good;--but now, so near the goal Of all my cherished hopes, I dare to speak. To-morrow's sun shall see her mine! no power Of hell can make us twain! With timid stealth No longer will I creep at dusky eve, To taste the golden fruits of Cupid's tree, And snatch a fearful, fleeting bliss: to-day With bright to-morrow shall be one! So smooth As runs the limpid brook, or silvery sand That marks the flight of time, our lives shall flow In continuity of joy!

Chorus (CAJETAN). Already Our hearts, my prince, with silent vows have blessed Thy happy love; and now from every tongue, For her--the royal, beauteous bride--should sound The glad acclaim; so tell what nook unseen, What deep umbrageous solitude, enshrines The charmer of thy heart? With magic spells Almost I deem she mocks our gaze, for oft In eager chase we scour each rustic path And forest dell; yet not a trace betrayed The lover's haunts, ne'er were the footsteps marked Of this mysterious fair.

DON MANUEL. The spell is broke! And all shall be revealed: now list my tale:-- 'Tis five months flown,--my father yet controlled The land, and bowed our necks with iron sway; Little I knew but the wild joys of arms, And mimic warfare of the chase;-- One day,-- Long had we tracked the boar with zealous toil On yonder woody ridge:--it chanced, pursuing A snow-white hind, far from your train I roved Amid the forest maze;--the timid beast, Along the windings of the narrow vale, Through rocky cleft and thick-entangled brake, Flew onward, scarce a moment lost, nor distant Beyond a javelin's throw; nearer I came not, Nor took an aim; when through a garden's gate, Sudden she vanished:--from my horse quick springing, I followed:--lo! the poor scared creature lay Stretched at the feet of a young, beauteous nun, That strove with fond caress of her fair hands To still its throbbing heart: wondering, I gazed; And motionless--my spear, in act to strike, High poised--while she, with her large piteous eyes For mercy sued--and thus we stood in silence Regarding one another. How long the pause I know not--time itself forgot;--it seemed Eternity of bliss: her glance of sweetness Flew to my soul; and quick the subtle flame Pervaded all my heart:-- But what I spoke, And how this blessed creature answered, none May ask; it floats upon my thought, a dream Of childhood's happy dawn! Soon as my sense Returned, I felt her bosom throb responsive To mine,--then fell melodious on my ear The sound, as of a convent bell, that called To vesper song; and, like some shadowy vision That melts in air, she flitted from my sight, And was beheld no more.

Chorus (CAJETAN). Thy story thrills My breast with pious awe! Prince, thou hast robbed The sanctuary, and for the bride of heaven Burned with unholy passion! Oh, remember The cloister's sacred vows!

DON MANUEL. Thenceforth one path My footsteps wooed; the fickle train was still Of young desires--new felt my being's aim, My soul revealed! and as the pilgrim turns His wistful gaze, where, from the orient sky, With gracious lustre beams Redemption's star;-- So to that brightest point of heaven, her presence, My hopes and longings centred all. No sun Sank in the western waves, but smiled farewell To two united lovers:--thus in stillness Our hearts were twined,--the all-seeing air above us Alone the faithful witness of our joys! Oh, golden hours! Oh, happy days! nor Heaven Indignant viewed our bliss;--no vows enchained Her spotless soul; naught but the link which bound it Eternally to mine! Chorus (CAJETAN). Those hallowed walls, Perchance the calm retreat of tender youth, No living grave?

DON MANUEL. In infant innocence Consigned a holy pledge, ne'er has she left Her cloistered home.

Chorus (CAJETAN). But what her royal line? The noble only spring from noble stem.

DON MANUEL. A secret to herself,--she ne'er has learned Her name or fatherland.

Chorus (CAJETAN). And not a trace Guides to her being's undiscovered springs?

DON MANUEL. An old domestic, the sole messenger Sent by her unknown mother, oft bespeaks her Of kingly race.

Chorus (CAJETAN). And hast thou won naught else From her garrulous age?

DON MANUEL. Too much I feared to peril My secret bliss!

Chorus (CAJETAN). What were his words? What tidings He bore--perchance thou know'st.

DON MANUEL. Oft he has cheered her With promise of a happier time, when all Shall be revealed.

Chorus (CAJETAN). Oh, say--betokens aught The time is near?

DON MANUEL. Not distant far the day That to the arms of kindred love once more Shall give the long forsaken, orphaned maid--Thus with mysterious words the aged man Has shadowed oft what most I dread--for awe Of change disturbs the soul supremely blest: Nay, more; but yesterday his message spoke The end of all my joys--this very dawn, He told, should smile auspicious on her fate, And light to other scenes--no precious hour Delayed my quick resolves--by night I bore her In secret to Messina.

Chorus (CAJETAN). Rash the deed Of sacrilegious spoil! forgive, my prince, The bold rebuke; thus to unthinking youth Old age may speak in friendship's warning voice.

DON MANUEL. Hard by the convent of the Carmelites, In a sequestered garden's tranquil bound, And safe from curious eyes, I left her,--hastening To meet my brother: trembling there she counts The slow-paced hours, nor deems how soon triumphant In queenly state, high on the throne of fame, Messina shall behold my timid bride. For next, encompassed by your knightly train, With pomp of greatness in the festal show, Her lover's form shall meet her wondering gaze! Thus will I lead her to my mother; thus-- While countless thousands on her passage wait Amid the loud acclaim--the royal bride Shall reach my palace gates!

Chorus (CAJETAN). Command us, prince, We live but to obey!

DON MANUEL. I tore myself Reluctant from her arms; my every thought Shall still be hers: so come along, my friends, To where the turbaned merchant spreads his store Of fabrics golden wrought with curious art; And all the gathered wealth of eastern climes. First choose the well-formed sandals--meet to guard And grace her delicate feet; then for her robe The tissue, pure as Etna's snow that lies Nearest the sunlight as the wreathy mist At summer dawn--so playful let it float About her airy limbs. A girdle next, Purple with gold embroidered o'er, to bind With witching grace the tunic that confines Her bosom's swelling charms: of silk the mantle,

Gorgeous with like empurpled hues, and fixed With clasp of gold--remember, too, the bracelets To gird her beauteous arms; nor leave the treasure Of ocean's pearly deeps and coral caves. About her locks entwine a diadem Of purest gems--the ruby's fiery glow Commingling with the emerald's green. A veil, From her tiara pendent to her feet, Like a bright fleecy cloud shall circle round Her slender form; and let a myrtle wreath Crown the enchanting whole! Chorus (CAJETAN). We haste, my prince. Amid the Bazar's glittering rows, to cull Each rich adornment.

DON MANUEL. From my stables lead A palfrey, milk-white as the steeds that draw The chariot of the sun; purple the housings, The bridle sparkling o'er with precious gems, For it shall bear my queen! Yourselves be ready With trumpet's cheerful clang, in martial train To lead your mistress home: let two attend me, The rest await my quick return; and each Guard well my secret purpose.

[He goes away accompanied by two of the CHORUS. Chorus (CAJETAN).

The princely strife is o'er, and say, What sport shall wing the slow-paced hours, And cheat the tedious day? With hope and fear's enlivening zest Disturb the slumber of the breast, And wake life's dull, untroubled sea With freshening airs of gay variety.

One of the Chorus (MANFRED).

Lovely is peace! A beauteous boy, Couched listless by the rivulet's glassy tide, 'Mid nature's tranquil scene, He views the lambs that skip with innocent joy, And crop the meadow's flowering pride:-- Then with his flute's enchanting sound, He wakes the mountain echoes round, Or slumbers in the sunset's ruddy sheen, Lulled by the murmuring melody. But war for me! my spirit's treasure, Its stern delight, and wilder pleasure: I love the peril and the pain, And revel in the surge of fortune's boisterous main!

A second (BERENGAR).

Is there not love, and beauty's smile That lures with soft, resistless wile? 'Tis thrilling hope! 'tis rapturous fear 'Tis heaven upon this mortal sphere; When at her feet we bend the knee, And own the glance of kindred ecstasy For ever on life's checkered way, 'Tis love that tints the darkening hues of care With soft benignant ray: The mirthful daughter of the wave, Celestial Venus ever fair, Enchants our happy spring with fancy's gleam, And wakes the airy forms of passion's golden dream.

First (MANFRED).

To the wild woods away! Quick let us follow in the train Of her, chaste huntress of the silver bow; And from the rocks amain Track through the forest gloom the bounding roe, The war-god's merry bride, The chase recalls the battle's fray, And kindles victory's pride:-- Up with the streaks of early morn, We scour with jocund hearts the misty vale, Loud echoing to the cheerful horn Over mountain--over dale-- And every languid sense repair, Bathed in the rushing streams of cold, reviving air.

Second (BERENGAR).

Or shall we trust the ever-moving sea, The azure goddess, blithe and free. Whose face, the mirror of the cloudless sky, Lures to her bosom wooingly? Quick let us build on the dancing waves A floating castle gay, And merrily, merrily, swim away! Who ploughs with venturous keel the brine Of the ocean crystalline-- His bride is fortune, the world his own, For him a harvest blooms unsown:-- Here, like the wind that swift careers The circling bound of earth and sky, Flits ever-changeful destiny! Of airy chance 'tis the sportive reign, And hope ever broods on the boundless main

A third (CAJETAN).

Nor on the watery waste alone Of the tumultuous, heaving sea;-- On the firm earth that sleeps secure, Based on the pillars of eternity. Say, when shall mortal joy endure? New bodings in my anxious breast, Waked by this sudden friendship, rise; Ne'er would I choose my home of rest On the stilled lava-stream, that cold Beneath the mountain lies Not thus was discord's flame controlled-- Too deep the rooted hate--too long They brooded in their sullen hearts O'er unforgotten, treasured wrong. In warning visions oft dismayed, I read the signs of coming woe; And now from this mysterious maid My bosom tells the dreaded ills shall flow: Unblest, I deem, the bridal chain Shall knit their secret loves, accursed With holy cloisters' spoil profane. No crooked paths to virtue lead; Ill fruit has ever sprung from evil seed!

BERENGAR. And thus to sad unhallowed rites Of an ill-omened nuptial tie, Too well ye know their father bore A bride of mournful destiny, Torn from his sire, whose awful curse has sped

Heaven's vengeance on the impious bed! This fierce, unnatural rage atones A parent's crime--decreed by fate, Their mother's offspring, strife and hate!

[The scene changes to a garden opening on the sea.

BEATRICE (steps forward from an alcove. She walks to and fro with an agitated air, looking round in every direction. Suddenly she stands still and listens). No! 'tis not he: 'twas but the playful wind Rustling the pine-tops.

To his ocean bed The sun declines, and with o'erwearied heart I count the lagging hours: an icy chill Creeps through my frame; the very solitude And awful silence fright my trembling soul! Where'er I turn naught meets my gaze--he leaves me Forsaken and alone! And like a rushing stream the city's hum Floats on the breeze, and dull the mighty sea Rolls murmuring to the rocks: I shrink to nothing With horrors compassed round; and like the leaf, Borne on the autumn blast, am hurried onward Through boundless space.

Alas! that e'er I left My peaceful cell--no cares, no fond desires Disturbed my breast, unruffled as the stream That glides in sunshine through the verdant mead: Nor poor in joys. Now--on the mighty surge Of fortune, tempest-tossed--the world enfolds me With giant arms! Forgot my childhood's ties I listened to the lover's flattering tale-- Listened, and trusted! From the sacred dome Allured--betrayed--for sure some hell-born magic Enchained my frenzied sense--I fled with him, The invader of religion's dread abodes! Where art thou, my beloved? Haste-- return-- With thy dear presence calm my struggling soul!

[She listens.

Hark! the sweet voice! No! 'twas the echoing surge That beats upon the shore; alas! he comes not. More faintly, o'er the distant waves, the sun Gleams with expiring ray; a deathlike shudder Creeps to my heart, and sadder, drearier grows E'en desolation's self. [She walks to and fro, and then listens again.

Yes! from the thicket shade A voice resounds! 'tis he! the loved one! No fond illusion mocks my listening ear. 'Tis louder--nearer: to his arms I fly-- To his breast!

[She rushes with outstretched arms to the extremity of the garden. DON CAESAR meets her.

DON CASAR. BEATRICE.

BEATRICE (starting back in horror) What do I see? [At the same moment the Chorus comes forward.

DON CAESAR. Angelic sweetness! fear not. [To the Chorus. Retire! your gleaming arms and rude array Affright the timorous maid. [To BEATRICE. Fear nothing! beauty And virgin shame are sacred in my eyes.

[The Chorus steps aside. He approaches and takes her hand.

Where hast thou been? for sure some envious power Has hid thee from my gaze: long have I sought thee: E'en from the hour when 'mid the funeral rites Of the dead prince, like some angelic vision, Lit with celestial brightness, on my sight Thou shonest, no other image in my breast Waking or dreaming, lives; nor to thyself Unknown thy potent spells; my glance of fire, My faltering accents, and my hand that lay Trembling in thine, bespoke my ecstasy! Aught else with solemn majesty the rite And holy place forbade: The bell proclaimed The awful sacrifice! With downcast eyes, And kneeling I adored: soon as I rose, And caught with eager gaze thy form again, Sudden it vanished; yet, with mighty magic Of love enchained, my spirit tracked thy presence; Nor ever, with unwearied quest, I cease At palace gates, amid the temple's throng, In secret paths retired, or public scenes, Where beauteous innocence perchance might rove, To mark each passing form--in vain; but, guided By some propitious deity this day One of my train, with happy vigilance, Espied thee in the neighboring church.

[BEATRICE, who had stood trembling with averted eyes, here makes a gesture of terror.

I see thee Once more; and may the spirit from this frame Be severed ere we part! Now let me snatch This glad, auspicious moment, and defy Or chance, or envious demon's power, to shake Henceforth my solid bliss; here I proclaim thee, Before this listening warlike train my bride, With pledge of knightly honors! [He shows her to the Chorus. Who thou art, I ask not: thou art mine! But that thy soul And birth are pure alike one glance informed My inmost heart; and though thy lot were mean, And poor thy lowly state, yet would I strain thee With rapture to my arms: no choice remains, Thou art my love--my wife! Know too, that lifted On fortune's height, I spurn control; my will Can raise thee to the pinnacle of greatness-- Enough my name--I am Don Caesar! None Is nobler in Messina!

[BEATRICE starts back in amazement. He remarks her agitation, and after a pause continues.

What a grace Lives in thy soft surprise and modest silence! Yes! gentle humbleness is beauty's crown-- The beautiful forever hid, and shrinking From its own lustre: but thy spirit needs Repose, for aught of strange--e'en sudden joy-- Is terror-fraught. I leave thee.

[Turning to the Chorus. From this hour She is your mistress, and my bride; so teach her With honors due to entertain the pomp Of queenly state. I will return with speed, And lead her home as fits Messina's princess.

[He goes away.

BEATRICE and the Chorus. Chorus (BOHEMUND). Fair maiden--hail to thee Thou lovely queen! Thine is the crown, and thine the victory! Of heroes to a distant age, The blooming mother thou shalt shine, Preserver of this kingly line.

(ROGER).

And thrice I bid thee hail, Thou happy fair! Sent in auspicious hour to bless This favored race--the god's peculiar care. Here twine the immortal wreaths of fame And evermore, from sire to son, Rolls on the sceptered sway, To heirs of old renown, a race of deathless name!

(BOHEMUND).

The household gods exultingly Thy coming wait; The ancient, honored sires, That on the portals frown sedate, Shall smile for thee! There blooming Hebe shall thy steps attend; And golden victory, that sits By Jove's eternal throne, with waving plumes For conquest ever spread, To welcome thee from heaven descend.

(ROGER.)

Ne'er from this queenly, bright array The crown of beauty fades, Departing to the realms of day, Each to the next, as good and fair, Extends the zone of feminine grace, And veil of purity:-- Oh, happy race! What vision glads my raptured eye! Equal in nature's blooming pride, I see the mother and the virgin bride.

BEATRICE (awaking from her reverie).

Oh, luckless hour! Alas! ill-fated maid! Where shall I fly From these rude warlike men? Lost and betrayed! A shudder o'er me came, When of this race accursed--the brothers twain-- Their hands embrued with kindred gore, I heard the dreaded name; Oft told, their strife and serpent hate With terror thrilled lay bosom's core:-- And now--oh, hapless fate! I tremble, 'mid the rage of discord thrown, Deserted and alone! [She runs into the alcove. Chorus (BOHEMUND).

Son of the immortal deities, And blest is he, the lord of power; His every joy the world can give; Of all that mortals prize He culls the flower.

(ROGER).

For him from ocean's azure caves The diver bears each pearl of purest ray; Whate'er from nature's boundless field Or toil or art has won, Obsequious at his feet we lay; His choice is ever free; We bow to chance, and fortune's blind decree.

(BOHEMUND.)

But this of princes' lot I deem The crowning treasure, joy supreme-- Of love the triumph and the prize, The beauty, star of neighboring eyes! She blooms for him alone, He calls the fairest maid his own.

(ROGER).

Armed for the deadly fray, The corsair bounds upon the strand, And drags, amid the gloom of night, away, The shrieking captive train, Of wild desires the hapless prey; But ne'er his lawless hands profane The gem--the peerless flower-- Whose charms shall deck the Sultan's bower.

(BOHEMUND.)

Now haste and watch, with curious eye, These hallowed precincts round, That no presumptuous foot come nigh The secret, solitary ground Guard well the maiden fair, Your chieftain's brightest jewel owns your care.

[The Chorus withdraws to the background. [The scene changes to a chamber in the interior of the palace. DONNA ISABELLA between DON MANUEL and DON CAESAR.

ISABELLA. The long-expected, festal day is come, My children's hearts are twined in one, as thus I fold their hands. Oh, blissful hour, when first A mother dares to speak in nature's voice, And no rude presence checks the tide of love. The clang of arms affrights mine ear no more; And as the owls, ill-omened brood of night, From some old, shattered homestead's ruined walls, Their ancient reign, fly forth a dusky swarm, Darkening the cheerful day; when absent long, The dwellers home return with joyous shouts, To build the pile anew; so Hate departs With all his grisly train; pale Envy, scowling Malice, And hollow-eyed Suspicion; from our gates, Hoarse murmuring, to the realms of night; while Peace, By Concord and fair Friendship led along, Comes smiling in his place. [She pauses. But not alone This day of joy to each restores a brother; It brings a sister!

Wonderstruck you gaze! Yet now the truth, in silence guarded long, Bursts from my soul. Attend! I have a daughter! A sister lives, ordained by heaven to bind ye With ties unknown before.

DON CAESAR. We have a sister! What hast thou said, my mother? never told Her being till this hour!

DON MANUEL. In childhood's years, Oft of a sister we have heard, untimely Snatched in her cradle by remorseless death; So ran the tale.

ISABELLA. She lives!

DON CAESAR. And thou wert silent!

ISABELLA. Hear how the seed was sown in early time, That now shall ripen to a joyful harvest. Ye bloomed in boyhood's tender age; e'en then By mutual, deadly hate, the bitter spring Of grief to this torn, anxious heart, dissevered; Oh, may your strife return no more! A vision, Strange and mysterious, in your father's breast Woke dire presage: it seemed that from his couch, With branches intertwined, two laurels grew, And in the midst a lily all in flames, That, catching swift the boughs and knotted stems, Burst forth with crackling rage, and o'er the house Spread in one mighty sea of fire: perplexed By this terrific dream, my husband sought An Arab, skilled to read the stars, and long The trusted oracle, whose counsels swayed His inmost purpose: thus the boding sage Spoke Fate's decrees: if I a daughter bore, Destruction to his sons and all his race From her should spring. Soon, by heaven's will, this child Of dreadful omen saw the light; your sire Commanded instant in the waves to throw The new-born innocent; a mother's love Prevailed, and, aided by a faithful servant, I snatched the babe from death.

DON CAESAR. Blest be the hands The ministers of thy care! Oh, ever rich Of counsels was a parent's love!

ISABELLA. But more Than Nature's mighty voice, a warning dream Impelled to save my child: while yet unborn She slumbered in my womb, sleeping I saw An infant, fair as of celestial kind, That played upon the grass; soon from the wood A lion rushed, and from his gory jaws, Caressing, in the infant's lap let fall His prey, new-caught; then through the air down swept An eagle, and with fond caress alike Dropped from his claws a trembling kid, and both Cowered at the infant's feet, a gentle pair. A monk, the saintly guide whose counsels poured In every earthly need, the balm of heaven Upon my troubled soul, my dream resolved. Thus spoke the man of God: a daughter, sent To knit the warring spirits of my sons In bonds of tender love, should recompense A mother's pains! Deep in my heart I treasured His words, and, reckless of the Pagan seer, Preserved the blessed child, ordained of heaven To still your growing strife; sweet pledge of hope And messenger of peace!

DON MANUEL (embracing his brother). There needs no sister To join our hearts; she shall but bind them closer.

ISABELLA. In a lone spot obscure, by stranger hands Nurtured, the secret flower has grown; to me Denied the joy to mark each infant charm And opening grace from that sad hour of parting; These arms ne'er clasped my child again! her sire, To jealousy's corroding fears a prey, And brooding dark suspicion, restless tracked Each day my steps. DON CAESAR. Yet three months flown, my father Sleeps in the tranquil grave; say, whence delayed The joyous tidings? Why so long concealed The maid, nor earlier taught our hearts to glow With brother's love?

ISABELLA. The cause, your frenzied hate, That raging unconfined, e'en on the tomb Of your scarce buried father, lit the flames Of mortal strife. What! could I throw my daughter Betwixt your gleaming blades? Or 'mid the storm Of passion would ye list a woman's counsels? Could she, sweet pledge of peace, of all our hopes The last and holy anchor, 'mid the rage Of discord find a home? Ye stand as brothers, So will I give a sister to your arms! The reconciling angel comes; each hour I wait my messenger's return; he leads her From her sequestered cell, to glad once more A mother's eyes.

DON MANUEL. Nor her alone this day Thy arms shall fold; joy pours through all our gates; Soon shall the desolate halls be full, the seat Of every blooming grace. Now hear my secret: A sister thou hast given; to thee I bring A daughter; bless thy son! My heart has found Its lasting shrine: ere this day's sun has set Don Manuel to thy feet shall lead his bride, The partner of his days.

ISABELLA. And to my breast With transport will I clasp the chosen maid That makes my first-born happy. Joy shall spring Where'er she treads, and every flower that blooms Around the path of life smile in her presence!

May bliss reward the son, that for my brows Has twined the choicest wreath a mother wears.

DON CAESAR. Yet give not all the fulness of thy blessing To him, thy eldest born. If love be blest, I, too, can give thee joy. I bring a daughter,

Another flower for thy most treasured garland! The maid that in this ice-cold bosom first Awoke the rapturous flame! Ere yonder sun Declines, Don Caesar's bride shall call thee mother.

DON MANUEL. Almighty Love! thou godlike power--for well We call thee sovereign of the breast! Thy sway Controls each warring element, and tunes To soft accord; naught lives but owns thy greatness. Lo! the rude soul that long defied thee melts At thy command! [He embraces DON CAESAR. Now I can trust thy heart, And joyful strain thee to a brother's arms! I doubt thy faith no more, for thou canst love!

ISABELLA. Thrice blest the day, when every gloomy care From my o'erlabored breast has flown. I see On steadfast columns reared our kingly race, And with contented spirit track the stream Of measureless time. In these deserted halls, Sad in my widow's veil, but yesterday Childless I roamed; and soon, in youthful charms Arrayed, three blooming daughters at my side Shall stand! Oh, happiest mother! Chief of women, In bliss supreme; can aught of earthly joy O'erbalance thine? But say, of royal stem, What maidens grace our isle? For ne'er my sons Would stoop to meaner brides.

DON MANUEL. Seek not to raise The veil that hides my bliss; another day Shall tell thee all. Enough--Don Manuel's bride Is worthy of thy son and thee.

ISABELLA. Thy sire Speaks in thy words; thus to himself retired Forever would he brood o'er counsels dark, And cloak his secret purpose;--your delay Be short, my son. [Turning to DON CAESAR. But thou--some royal maid, Daughter of kings, hath stirred thy soul to love; So speak—her name----

DON CAESAR. I have no art to veil My thoughts with mystery's garb--my spirit free And open as my brows; which thou wouldst know Concerned me never. What illumes above Heaven's flaming orb? Himself! On all the world He shines, and with his beaming glory tells From light he sprung:--in her pure eyes I gazed, I looked into her heart of hearts:--the brightness Revealed the pearl. Her race--her name--my mother, Ask not of me!

ISABELLA. My son, explain thy words, For, like some voice divine, the sudden charm Has thralled thy soul: to deeds of rash emprise Thy nature prompted, not to fantasies Of boyish love:--tell me, what swayed thy choice? DON CAESAR. My choice? my mother! Is it choice when man Obeys the might of destiny, that brings The awful hour? I sought no beauteous bride, No fond delusion stirred my tranquil breast, Still as the house of death; for there, unsought, I found the treasure of my soul. Thou know'st That, heedless ever of the giddy race, I looked on beauty's charms with cold disdain, Nor deemed of womankind there lived another Like thee--whom my idolatrous fancy decked With heavenly graces:-- 'Twas the solemn rite Of my dead father's obsequies; we stood Amid the countless throng, with strange attire Hid from each other's glance; for thus ordained Thy thoughtful care lest with outbursting rage, E' en by the holy place unawed, our strife Should mar the funeral pomp. With sable gauze The nave was all o'erhung; the altar round Stood twenty giant saints, uplifting each A torch; and in the midst reposed on high The coffin, with o'erspreading pall, that showed, In white, redemption's sign;--thereon were laid The staff of sovereignty, the princely crown, The golden spurs of knighthood, and the sword, With diamond-studded belt:-- And all was hushed In silent prayer, when from the lofty choir, Unseen, the pealing organ spoke, and loud From hundred voices burst the choral strain! Then, 'mid the tide of song, the coffin sank With the descending floor beneath, forever Down to the world below:-- but, wide outspread Above the yawning grave, the pall upheld The gauds of earthly state, nor with the corpse To darkness fell; yet on the seraph wings Of harmony, the enfranchised spirit soared To heaven and mercy's throne: Thus to thy thought, My mother, I have waked the scene anew, And say, if aught of passion in my breast Profaned the solemn hour; yet then the beams Of mighty love--so willed my guiding star-- First lit my soul; but how it chanced, myself I ask in vain.

ISABELLA. I would hear all; so end Thy tale.

DON CAESAR. What brought her to my side, or whence She came, I know not:--from her presence quick Some secret all-pervading inward charm Awoke; 'twas not the magic of a smile, Nor playful Cupid in her cheeks, nor more, The form of peerless grace;--'twas beauty's soul, The speaking virtue, modesty inborn, That as with magic spells, impalpable To sense, my being thralled. We breathed together The air of heaven:--enough!--no utterance asked Of words, our spiritual converse;--in my heart, Though strange, yet with familiar ties inwrought She seemed, and instant spake the thought--'tis she! Or none that lives!

DON MANUEL (interposing with eagerness). That is the sacred fire From heaven! the spark of love--that on the soul Bursts like the lightning's flash, and mounts in flame, When kindred bosoms meet! No choice remains-- Who shall resist? What mortal break the band That heaven has knit?

Brother, my blissful fortune Was echoed in thy tale--well thou hast raised The veil that shadows yet my secret love.

ISABELLA. Thus destiny has marked the wayward course Of my two sons: the mighty torrent sweeps Down from the precipice; with rage he wears His proper bed, nor heeds the channel traced By art and prudent care. So to the powers That darkly sway the fortunes of our house, Trembling I yield. One pledge of hope remains; Great as their birth-- their noble souls.

ISABELLA, DON MANUEL, DON CAESAR. DIEGO is seen at the door.

ISABELLA. But see, My faithful messenger returns. Come near me, Honest Diego. Quick! Where is she? Tell me, Where is my child? There is no secret here. Oh, speak! No longer from my eyes conceal her; Come! we are ready for the height of joy.

[She is about to lead him towards the door.

What means this pause? Thou lingerest--thou art dumb-- Thy looks are terror-fraught--a shudder creeps Through all my frame--declare thy tidings!--speak! Where is she? Where is Beatrice?

[She is about to rush from the chamber.

DON MANUEL (to himself abstractedly). Beatrice! DIEGO (holding back the PRINCESS). Be still!

ISABELLA. Where is she? Anguish tears my breast! DIEGO. She comes not. I bring no daughter to thy arms.

ISABELLA. Declare Thy message! Speak! by all the saints! What has befallen?

DON MANUEL. Where is my sister? Tell us, Thou harbinger of ill!

DIEGO. The maid is stolen By corsairs! lost! Oh! that I ne'er had seen This day of woe!

DON MANUEL. Compose thyself, my mother! DON CAESAR. Be calm; list all this tale.

DIEGO. At thy command I sought in haste the well-known path that leads To the old sanctuary:--joy winged my footsteps; The journey was my last!

DON CAESAR. Be brief! DON MANUEL. Proceed!

DIEGO. Soon as I trod the convent's court--impatient-- I ask-- "Where is thy daughter?" Terror sate In every eye; and straight, with horror mute, I heard the worst.

[ISABELLA sinks, pale and trembling, upon a chair; DON MANUEL is busied about her.

DON CAESAR. Say'st thou by pirates stolen? Who saw the band?--what tongue relates the spoil?

DIEGO. Not far a Moorish galley was descried, At anchor in the bay---- DON CAESAR. The refuge oft From tempests' rage; where is the bark? DIEGO. At down, With favoring breeze she stood to sea. DON CAESAR. But never One prey contents the Moor; say, have they told Of other spoil?

DIEGO. A herd that pastured near Was dragged away.

DON CAESAR. Yet from the convent's bound How tear the maid unseen? DIEGO. 'Tis thought with ladders They scaled the wall.

DON CAESAR. Thou knowest what jealous care Enshrines the bride of Heaven; scarce could their steps Invade the secret cells.

DIEGO. Bound by no vows The maiden roved at will; oft would she seek Alone the garden's shade. Alas! this day, Ne'er to return!

DON CAESAR. Saidst thou--the prize of corsairs? Perchance, at other bidding, she forsook The sheltering dome----

ISABELLA (rising suddenly). 'Twas force! 'twas savage spoil! Ne'er has my child, reckless of honor's ties With vile seducer fled! My sons! Awake! I thought to give a sister to your arms; I ask a daughter from your swords! Arise! Avenge this wrong! To arms! Launch every ship! Scour all our coasts! From sea to sea pursue them! Oh, bring my daughter! haste!

DON CAESAR. Farewell--I fly To vengeance! [He goes away.

[DON MANUEL arouses himself from a state of abstraction, and turns, with an air of agitation, to DIEGO.

DON MANUEL. Speak! within the convent's walls When first unseen---- DIEGO. This day at dawn.

DON MANUEL (to ISABELLA). Her name Thou say'st is Beatrice? ISABELLA. No question! Fly! DON MANUEL. Yet tell me---- ISABELLA. Haste! Begone! Why this delay? Follow thy brother. DON MANUEL. I conjure thee--speak----

ISABELLA (dragging him away). Behold my tears!

DON MANUEL. Where was she hid? What region Concealed my sister?

ISABELLA. Scarce from curious eyes In the deep bosom of the earth more safe My child had been!

DIEGO. Oh! now a sudden horror Starts in my breast. DON MANUEL. What gives thee fear?

DIEGO. 'Twas I That guiltless caused this woe! ISABELLA. Unhappy man! What hast thou done?

DIEGO. To spare thy mother's heart One anxious pang, my mistress, I concealed What now my lips shall tell: 'twas on the day When thy dead husband in the silent tomb Was laid; from every side the unnumbered throng Pressed eager to the solemn rites; thy daughter-- For e'en amid the cloistered shade was noised The funeral pomp, urged me, with ceaseless prayers, To lead her to the festival of Death. In evil hour I gave consent; and, shrouded In sable weeds of mourning, she surveyed Her father's obsequies. With keen reproach My bosom tells (for through the veil her charms Resistless shone), 'twas there, perchance, the spoiler Lurked to betray.

DON MANUEL (to himself). Thrice happy words! I live! It was another! ISABELLA (to DIEGO). Faithless! Ill betide Thy treacherous age!

DIEGO. Oh, never have I strayed From duty's path! My mistress, in her prayers I heard the voice of Nature; thus from Heaven Ordained,--methought, the secret impulse moves Of kindred blood, to hallow with her tears A father's grave: the tender office owned Thy servant's care, and thus with good intent I wrought but ill.

DON MANUEL (to himself). Why stand I thus a prey To torturing fears! No longer will I bear The dread suspense---I will know all!

DON CAESAR (who returns). Forgive me, I follow thee. DON MANUEL. Away! Let no man follow.

[Exit.

DON CAESAR (looking after him in surprise). What means my brother? Speak----

ISABELLA. In wonder lost I gaze; some mystery lurks----

DON CAESAR. Thou mark'st, my mother, My quick return; with eager zeal I flew At thy command, nor asked one trace to guide My footsteps to thy daughter. Whence was torn Thy treasure? Say, what cloistered solitude Enshrined the beauteous maid?

ISABELLA. 'Tis consecrate To St. Cecilia; deep in forest shades, Beyond the woody ridge that slowly climbs Toward's Etna's towering throne, it seems a refuge Of parted souls!

DON CAESAR. Have courage, trust thy sons; She shall be thine, though with unwearied quest O'er every land and sea I track her presence To earth's extremest bounds: one thought alone Disturbs,--in stranger hands my timorous bride Waits my return; to thy protecting arms I give the pledge of all my joy! She comes; Soon on her faithful bosom thou shalt rest In sweet oblivion of thy cares. [Exit.

ISABELLA. When will the ancient curse be stilled that weighs Upon our house? Some mocking demon sports With every new-formed hope, nor envious leaves One hour of joy. So near the haven smiled-- So smooth the treacherous main--secure I deemed My happiness: the storm was lulled; and bright In evening's lustre gleamed the sunny shore! Then through the placid air the tempest sweeps, And bears me to the roaring surge again!

[She goes into the interior of the palace, followed by DIEGO. The Scene changes to the Garden.

Both Choruses, afterwards BEATRICE.

The Chorus of DON MANUEL enters in solemn procession, adorned with garlands, and bearing the bridal ornaments above mentioned. The Chorus of DON CAESAR opposes their entrance.

First Chorus (CAJETAN). Begone!

Second Chorus (BOHEMUND). Not at thy bidding! CAJETAN. Seest thou not Thy presence irks?

BOHEMUND. Thou hast it, then, the longer! CAJETAN. My place is here! What arm repels me? BOHEMUND, Mine!

CAJETAN. Don Manuel sent me hither. BOHEMUND. I obey My Lord Don Caesar.

CAJETAN. To the eldest born Thy master reverence owes. BOHEMUND. The world belongs To him that wins!

CAJETAN. Unmannered knave, give place! BOHEMUND. Our swords be measured first! CAJETAN. I find thee ever A serpent in my path. BOHEMUND. Where'er I list Thus will I meet thee! CAJETAN. Say, why cam'st thou hither To spy?---- BOHEMUND. And thou to question and command? CAJETAN. To parley I disdain!

BOHEMUND. Too much I grace thee By words!

CAJETAN. Thy hot, impetuous youth should bow To reverend age. BOHEMUND. Older thou art--not braver.

BEATRICE (rushing from her place of concealment). Alas! What mean these warlike men?

CAJETAN (to BOHEMUND). I heed not Thy threats and lofty mien. BOHEMUND. I serve a master Better than thine.

BEATRICE. Alas! Should he appear!

CAJETAN. Thou liest! Don Manuel thousandfold excels.

BOHEMUND. In every strife the wreath of victory decks Don Caesar's brows!

BEATRICE. Now he will come! Already The hour is past! CAJETAN. 'Tis peace, or thou shouldst know My vengeance! BOHEMUND. Fear, not peace, thy arm refrains. BEATRICE. Oh! Were he thousand miles remote!

CAJETAN. Thy looks But move my scorn; the compact I obey. BOHEMUND. The coward's ready shield!

CAJETAN. Come on! I follow. BOHEMUND. To arms!

BEATRICE (in the greatest agitation). Their falchions gleam-- the strife begins! Ye heavenly powers, his steps refrain! Some snare Throw round his feet, that in this hour of dread He come not: all ye angels, late implored To give him to my arms, reverse my prayers; Far, far from hence convey the loved one!

[She runs into the alcove. At the moment when the two Choruses are about to engage, DON MANUEL appears.

DON MANUEL, the Chorus. DON MANUEL. What do I see!

First Chorus to the Second (CAJETAN, BERENGAR, MANFRED). Come on! Come on!

Second Chorus (BOHEMUND, ROGER, HIPPOLYTE). Down with them! DON MANUEL (stepping between them with drawn sword). Hold!

33

CAJETAN. 'Tis the prince! BOHEMUND. Be still! DON MANUEL. I stretch him dead Upon this verdant turf that with one glance Of scorn prolongs the strife, or threats his foe! Why rage ye thus? What maddening fiend impels To blow the flames of ancient hate anew, Forever reconciled? Say, who began The conflict? Speak----

First Chorus (CAJETAN, BERENGAR). My prince, we stood---- Second Chorus (ROGER, BOHEMUND) interrupting them. They came DON MANUEL (to the First Chorus). Speak thou!

First Chorus (CAJETAN). With wreaths adorned, in festal train, We bore the bridal gifts; no thought of ill Disturbed our peaceful way; composed forever With holy pledge of love we deemed your strife, And trusting came; when here in rude array Of arms encamped they stood, and loud defied us!

DON MANUEL. Slave! Is no refuge safe? Shall discord thus Profane the bower of virgin innocence, The home of sanctity and peace? [To the Second Chorus. Retire-- Your warlike presence ill beseems; away! I would be private. [They hesitate. In your master's name I give command; our souls are one, our lips Declare each other's thoughts; begone! [To the First Chorus. Remain! And guard the entrance.

BOHEMUND. So! What next? Our masters Are reconciled; that's plain; and less he wins Of thanks than peril, that with busy zeal In princely quarrel stirs; for when of strife His mightiness aweary feels, of guilt He throws the red-dyed mantle unconcerned On his poor follower's luckless head, and stands Arrayed in virtue's robes! So let them end E'en as they will their brawls, I hold it best That we obey.

[Exit Second Chorus. The first withdraws to the back of the stage; at the same moment BEATRICE rushes forward, and throws herself into DON MANUEL'S arms. BEATRICE. 'Tis thou! Ah! cruel one, Again I see thee--clasp thee--long appalled, To thousand ills a prey, trembling I languish For thy return: no more--in thy loved arms I am at peace, nor think of dangers past, Thy breast my shield from every threatening harm. Quick! Let us fly! they see us not!--away! Nor lose the moment. Ha! Thy looks affright me! Thy sullen, cold reserve! Thou tear'st thyself Impatient from my circling arms, I know thee No more! Is this Don Manuel? My beloved? My husband?

DON MANUEL. Beatrice!

BEATRICE. No words! The moment Is precious! Haste. DON MANUEL. Yet tell me----

BEATRICE. Quick! Away! Ere those fierce men return. DON MANUEL. Be calm, for naught Shall trouble thee of ill. BEATRICE. Oh, fly! alas, Thou know'st them not!

DON MANUEL. Protected by this arm Canst thou fear aught? BEATRICE. Oh, trust me; mighty men Are here!

DON MANUEL. Beloved! mightier none than I! BEATRICE. And wouldst thou brave this warlike host alone? DON MANUEL. Alone! the men thou fear'st---- BEATRICE. Thou know'st them not, Nor whom they serve.

DON MANUEL. Myself! I am their lord!

BEATRICE. Thou art--a shudder creeps through all my frame! DON MANUEL. Far other than I seemed; learn at last To know me, Beatrice. Not the poor knight Am I, the stranger and unknown, that loving Taught thee to love; but what I am--my race-- My power----

BEATRICE. And art thou not Don Manuel? Speak-- Who art thou?

DON MANUEL. Chief of all that bear the name, I am Don Manuel, Prince of Messina!

BEATRICE. Art thou Don Manuel, Don Caesar's brother? DON MANUEL. Don Caesar is my brother.

BEATRICE. Is thy brother!

DON MANUEL. What means this terror? Know'st thou, then, Don Caesar? None other of my race?

BEATRICE. Art thou Don Manuel, That with thy brother liv'st in bitter strife Of long inveterate hate?

DON MANUEL. This very sun Smiled on our glad accord! Yes, we are brothers! Brothers in heart!

BEATRICE. And reconciled? This day?

DON MANUEL. What stirs this wild disorder? Hast thou known Aught but our name? Say, hast thou told me all? Is there no secret? Hast thou naught concealed? Nothing disguised?

BEATRICE. Thy words are dark; explain, What shall I tell thee?

DON MANUEL. Of thy mother naught Hast thou e'er told; who is she? If in words I paint her, bring her to thy sight----

BEATRICE. Thou know'st her! And thou wert silent! DON MANUEL. If I know thy mother, Horrors betide us both!

BEATRICE. Oh, she is gracious As the sun's orient beam! Yes! I behold her; Fond memory wakes;--and from my bosom's depths Her godlike presence rises to my view! I see around her snowy neck descend The tresses of her raven hair, that shade The form of sculptured loveliness; I see The pale, high-thoughted brow; the darkening glance Of her large lustrous orbs; I hear the tones Of soul-fraught sweetness!

DON MANUEL. 'Tis herself!

BEATRICE. This day, Perchance had give me to her arms, and knit Our souls in everlasting love;--such bliss I have renounced, yes! I have lost a mother For thee!

DON MANUEL. Console thyself, Messina's princess Henceforth shall call thee daughter; to her feet I lead thee; come--she waits. What hast thou said?

BEATRICE. Thy mother and Don Caesar's? Never! never!

DON MANUEL. Thou shudderest! Whence this horror? Hast thou known My mother? Speak----

BEATRICE. O grief! O dire misfortune! Alas! that e'er I live to see this day!

DON MANUEL. What troubles thee? Thou know'st me, thou hast found, In the poor stranger knight, Messina's prince!

BEATRICE. Give me the dear unknown again! With him On earth's remotest wilds I could be blest!

DON CAESAR (behind the scene). Away! What rabble throng is here? BEATRICE. That voice! Oh heavens! Where shall I fly! DON MANUEL. Know'st thou that voice? No! thou hast never heard it; to thine ear 'Tis strange----

BEATRICE. Oh, come--delay not----

DON MANUEL. Wherefore I fly? It is my brother's voice! He seeks me--how He tracked my steps----

BEATRICE. By all the holy saints! Brave not his wrath! oh quit this place--avoid him-- Meet not thy brother here!

DON MANUEL. My soul! thy fears Confound; thou hear'st me not; our strife is o'er. Yes! we are reconciled.

BEATRICE. Protect me, heaven, In this dread hour!

DON MANUEL. A sudden dire presage Starts in my breast--I shudder at the thought: If it be true! Oh, horror! Could she know That voice! Wert thou--my tongue denies to utter The words of fearful import--Beatrice! Say, wert thou present at the funeral rites Of my dead sire?

BEATRICE. Alas!

DON MANUEL. Thou wert! BEATRICE. Forgive me!

DON MANUEL. Unhappy woman! BEATRICE. I was present!

DON MANUEL. Horror!

BEATRICE. Some mighty impulse urged me to the scene-- Oh, be not angry--to thyself I owned The ardent fond desire; with darkening brow Thou listened'st to my prayer, and I was silent, But what misguiding inauspicious star Allured, I know not; from my inmost soul The wish, the dear emotion spoke; and vain Aught else:--Diego gave consent--oh, pardon me! I disobeyed thee.

[She advances towards him imploringly; at the same moment DON CAESAR enters, accompanied by the whole Chorus.

BOTH BROTHERS, BOTH CHORUSES, BEATRICE.

Second Chorus (BOHEMUND) to DON CAESAR. Thou heliev'st us not-- Believe thine eyes!

DON CAESAR (rushes forward furiously, and at the sight of his brother starts back with horror). Some hell-born magic cheats My senses; in her arms! Envenomed snake! Is this thy love? For this thy treacherous heart Could lure with guise of friendship! Oh, from heaven Breathed my immortal hate! Down, down to hell, Thou soul of falsehood!

[He stabs him, DON MANUEL falls.

DON MANUEL. Beatrice!--my brother! I die! [Dies. BEATRICE sinks lifeless at his side.

First Chorus (CAJETAN). Help! Help! To arms! Avenge with blood The bloody deed!

Second Chorus (BOHEMUND). The fortune of the day Is ours! The strife forever stilled:--Messina Obeys one lord.

First Chorus (CAJETAN, BERENGAR, MANFRED). Revenge! The murderer Shall die! Quick, offer to your master's shade Appeasing sacrifice!

Second Chorus (BOHEMUND, ROGER, HIPPOLYTE). My prince! fear nothing, Thy friends are true. DON CAESAR (steps between them, looking around). Be still! The foe is slain That practised on my trusting, honest heart With snares of brother's love. Oh, direful shows The deed of death! But righteous heaven hath judged.

First Chorus (CAJETAN). Alas to thee, Messina! Woe forever! Sad city! From thy blood-stained walls this deed Of nameless horror taints the skies; ill fare Thy mothers and thy children, youth and age, And offspring yet, unborn!

DON CAESAR. Too late your grief-- Here give your help. [Pointing to BEATRICE. Call her to life, and quick Depart this scene of terror and of death. I must away and seek my sister:--Hence! Conduct her to my mother-- And tell her that her son, Don Caesar, sends her!

[Exit.

[The senseless BEATRICE is placed on a litter and carried away by the Second Chorus. The First Chorus remains with the body, round which the boys who bear the bridal presents range themselves in a semicircle.

Chorus (CAJETAN).

List, how with dreaded mystery Was signed to my prophetic soul, Of kindred blood the dire decree:-- Hither with noiseless, giant stride I saw the hideous fiend of terror glide! 'Tis past! I strive not to control My shuddering awe--so swift of ill The Fates the warning sign fulfil. Lo! to my sense dismayed, Sudden the deed of death has shown Whate'er my boding fears portrayed. The visioned thought was pain; The present horror curdles every vein

One of the Chorus (MANFRED).

Sound, sound the plaint of woe! Beautiful youth! Outstretched and pale he lies, Untimely cropped in early bloom; The heavy night of death has sealed his eyes;-- In this glad hour of nuptial joy, Snatched by relentless doom, He sleeps--while echoing to the sky, Of sorrow bursts the loud, despairing cry! A second (CAJETAN).

We come, we come, in festal pride, To greet the beauteous bride; Behold! the nuptial gifts, the rich attire The banquet waits, the guests are there; They bid thee to the solemn rite Of hymen quick repair. Thou hear'st them not--the sportive lyre, The frolic dance, shall ne'er invite; Nor wake thee from thy lowly bed, For deep the slumber of the dead!

The whole Chorus.

No more the echoing horn shall cheer Nor bride with tones of sweetness charm his ear. On the cold earth he lies, In death's eternal slumber closed his eyes.

A third (CAJETAN).

What are the hopes, and fond desires Of mortals' transitory race? This day, with harmony of voice and soul, Ye woke the long-extinguished fires Of brothers' love--yon flaming orb Lit with his earliest beams your dear embrace At eve, upon the gory sand Thou liest--a reeking corpse! Stretched by a brother's murderous hand. Vain projects, treacherous hopes, Child of the fleeting hour are thine; Fond man! thou rear'st on dust each bold design,

Chorus (BERENGAR).

To thy mother I will bear The burden of unutterable woe! Quick shall yon cypress, blooming fair, Bend to the axe's murderous blow Then twine the mournful bier! For ne'er with verdant life the tree shall smile That grew on death's devoted soil; Ne'er in the breeze the branches play, Nor shade the wanderer in the noontide ray; 'Twas marked to bear the fruits of doom, Cursed to the service of the tomb.

First (CAJETAN). Woe to the murderer! Woe That sped exulting in his pride, Behold! the parched earth drinks the crimson tide. Down, down it flows, unceasingly, To the dim caverned halls below, Where throned in kindred gloom the sister train, Of Themis progeny severe, Brood in their songless, silent reign! Stern minister of wrath's decree, They catch in swarthy cups thy streaming gore, And pledge with horrid rites for vengeance evermore.

Second (BERENGAR).

Though swift of deed the traces fade From earth, before the enlivening ray; As o'er the brow the transient shade Of thought, the hues of fancy flit away:-- Yet in the mystic womb unseen, Of the dark ruling hours that sway Our mortal lot, whate'er has been, With new creative germ defies decay.

The blooming field is time For nature's ever-teeming shoot, And all is seed, and all is fruit.

[The Chorus goes away, bearing the corpse of DON MANUEL on a bier. SCENE--The hall of pillars. It is night.

The stage is lighted from above by a single large lamp. DONNA ISABELLA and DIEGO advance to the front.

ISABELLA. As yet no joyful tidings, not a trace Found of the lost one!

DIEGO. Nothing have we heard, My mistress; yet o'er every track, unwearied, Thy sons pursue. Ere long the rescued maid Shall smile at dangers past.

ISABELLA. Alas! Diego, My heart is sad; 'twas I that caused this woe! DIEGO. Vex not thy anxious bosom; naught escaped Thy thoughtful care. ISABELLA. Oh! had I earlier shown The hidden treasure! DIEGO. Prudent were thy counsels, Wisely thou left'st her in retirement's shade; So, trust in heaven.

ISABELLA. Alas! no joy is perfect Without this chance of ill my bliss were pure.

DIEGO. Thy happiness is but delayed; enjoy The concord of thy sons.

ISABELLA. The sight was rapture Supreme, when, locked in one another's arms, They glowed with brothers' love.

DIEGO. And in the heart It burns; for ne'er their princely souls have stooped To mean disguise.

ISABELLA. Now, too, their bosoms wake To gentler thoughts, and own their softening sway Of love. No more their hot, impetuous youth Revels in liberty untamed, and spurns Restraint of law, attempered passion's self, With modest, chaste reserve. To thee, Diego, I will unfold my secret heart; this hour Of feeling's opening bloom, expected long, Wakes boding fears: thou know'st to sudden rage Love stirs tumultuous breasts; and if this flame With jealousy should rouse the slumbering fires Of ancient hate--I shudder at the thought! If these discordant souls perchance have thrilled In fatal unison! Enough; the clouds That black with thundering menace o'er me hung Are past; some angel sped them tranquil by, And my enfranchised spirit breathes again.

DIEGO. Rejoice, my mistress; for thy gentle sense And soft, prevailing art more weal have wrought Than all thy husband's power. Be praise to thee And thy auspicious star!

ISABELLA. Yes, fortune smiled; Nor light the task, so long with apt disguise To veil the cherished secret of my heart, And cheat my ever-jealous lord: more hard To stifle mighty nature's pleading voice, That, like a prisoned fire, forever strove To rend its confines. DIEGO. All shall yet be well; Fortune, propitious to our hopes, gave pledge Of bliss that time will show.

ISABELLA. I praise not yet My natal star, while darkening o'er my fate This mystery hangs: too well the dire mischance Tells of the fiend whose never-slumbering rage Pursues our house. Now list what I have done, And praise or blame me as thou wilt; from thee My bosom guards no secret: ill I brook This dull repose, while swift o'er land and sea My sons unwearied, track their sister's flight, Yes, I have sought; heaven counsels oft, when vain All mortal aid.

DIEGO. What I may know, my mistress, Declare.

ISABELLA. On Etna's solitary height A reverend hermit dwells,--benamed of old The mountain seer,--who to the realms of light More near abiding than the toilsome race Of mortals here below, with purer air Has cleansed each earthly, grosser sense away; And from the lofty peak of gathered years, As from his mountain home, with downward glance Surveys the crooked paths of worldly strife. To him are known the fortunes of our house; Oft has the holy sage besought response From heaven, and many a curse with earnest prayer Averted: thither at my bidding flew, On wings of youthful haste, a messenger, To ask some tidings of my child: each hour I wait his homeward footsteps.

DIEGO. If mine eyes Deceive me not, he comes; and well his speed Has earned thy praise.

MESSENGER, ISABELLA, DIEGO.

ISABELLA (to MESSENGER). Now speak, and nothing hide Of weal or woe; be truth upon thy lips! What tidings bear'st thou from the mountain seer?

MESSENGER. His answer: "Quick! retrace thy steps; the lost one Is found." ISABELLA. Auspicious tongue! Celestial sounds Of peace and joy! thus ever to my vows. Thrice honored sage, thy kindly message spoke! But say, which heaven-directed brother traced My daughter?

MESSENGER. 'Twas thy eldest born that found The deep-secluded maid.

ISABELLA. Is it Don Manuel That gives her to my arms? Oh, he was ever The child of blessing! Tell me, hast thou borne My offering to the aged man? the tapers To burn before his saint? for gifts, the prize Of worldly hearts, the man of God disdains.

MESSENGER. He took the torches from my hands in silence And stepping to the altar--where the lamp Burned to his saint--illumed them at his fire, And instant set in flames the hermit cell, Where he has honored God these ninety years!

ISABELLA. What hast thou said? What horrors fright my soul?

MESSENGER. And three times shrieking "Woe!" with downward course, He fled; but silent with uplifted arm Beckoned me not to follow, nor regard him So hither I have hastened, terror-sped.

ISABELLA. Oh, I am tossed amid the surge again Of doubt and anxious fears; thy tale appals With ominous sounds of ill. My daughter found-- Thou sayest; and by my eldest born, Don Manuel? The tidings ne'er shall bless, that heralded This deed of woe!

MESSENGER. My mistress! look around Behold the hermit's message to thine eyes Fulfilled. Some charm deludes my sense, or hither Thy daughter comes, girt by the warlike train Of thy two sons!

[BEATRICE is carried in by the Second Chorus on a litter, and placed in the front of the stage. She is still without perception, and motionless.

ISABELLA, DIEGO, MESSENGER, BEATRICE. Chorus (BOHEMUND, ROGER, HIPPOLYTE, and the other nine followers of DON CAESAR.)

Chorus (BOHEMUND). Here at thy feet we lay The maid, obedient to our lord's command: 'Twas thus he spoke--"Conduct her to my mother; And tell her that her son, Don Caesar, sends her!"

ISABELLA (is advancing towards her with outstretched arms, and starts back in horror). Heavens! she is motionless and pale!

Chorus (BOHEMUND). She lives, She will awake, but give her time to rouse From the dread shock that holds each sense enthralled.

ISABELLA. My daughter! Child of all my cares and pains! And is it thus I see thee once again? Thus thou returnest to thy father's halls! Oh, let my breath relume thy vital spark; Yes! I will strain thee to a mother's arms And hold thee fast--till from the frost of death Released thy life-warm current throbs again.

[To the Chorus.

Where hast thou found her? Speak! What dire mischance Has caused this sight of woe?

Chorus (BOHEMUND). My lips are dumb! Ask not of me: thy son will tell thee all-- Don Caesar--for 'tis he that sends her.

ISABELLA 'Tell me Would'st thou not say Don Manuel? Chorus (BOHEMUND). 'Tis Don Caesar That sends her to thee.

ISABELLA (to the MESSENGER). How declared the Seer? Speak! Was it not Don Manuel?

MESSENGER. 'Twas he! Thy elder born. ISABELLA. Be blessings on his head Which e'er it be; to him I owe a daughter, Alas! that in this blissful hour, so long Expected, long implored, some envious fiend Should mar my joy! Oh, I must stem the tide Of nature's transport! In her childhood's home I see my daughter; me she knows not--heeds not-- Nor answers to a mother's voice of love Ope, ye dear eyelids--hands be warm--and heave Thou lifeless bosom with responsive throbs To mine! 'Tis she! Diego, look! 'tis Beatrice! The long-concealed--the lost-- the rescued one! Before the world I claim her for my own!

Chorus (BOHEMUND). New signs of terror to my boding soul Are pictured;--in amazement lost I stand! What light shall pierce this gloom of mystery?

ISABELLA (to the Chorus, who exhibit marks of confusion and embarrassment). Oh, ye hard hearts! Ye rude unpitying men! A mother's transport from your breast of steel Rebounds, as from the rocks the heaving surge! I look around your train, nor mark one glance Of soft regard. Where are my sons? Oh, tell me Why come they not, and from their beaming eyes Speak comfort to my soul? For here environed I stand amid the desert's raging brood, Or monsters of the deep!

DIEGO. She opes her eyes! She moves! She lives! ISABELLA. She lives! On me be thrown Her earliest glance! DIEGO. See! They are closed again-- She shudders!

ISABELLA (to the Chorus). Quick! Retire--your aspect frights her. [Chorus steps back.

RORER. Well pleased I shun her sight.

DIEGO. With outstretched eyes, And wonderstruck, she seems to measure thee. BEATRICE. Not strange those lineaments--where am I? ISABELLA. Slowly Her sense returns.

DIEGO. Behold! upon her knees She sinks. BEATRICE. Oh, angel visage of my mother! ISABELLA. Child of my heart!

BEATRICE. See! kneeling at thy feet The guilty one! ISABELLA. I hold thee in my arms! Enough--forgotten all! DIEGO. Look in my face, Canst thou remember me?

BEATRICE. The reverend brows Of honest old Diego! ISABELLA. Faithful guardian Of thy young years.

BEATRICE. And am I once again With kindred? ISABELLA. Naught but death shall part us more! BEATRICE. Will thou ne'er send me to the stranger? ISABELLA. Never! Fate is appeased.

BEATRICE. And am I next thy heart? And was it all a dream--a hideous dream? My mother! at my feet he fell! I know not What brought me hither--yet 'tis well. Oh, bliss! That I am safe in thy protecting arms; They would have ta'en me to the princess, mother-- Sooner to death!

ISABELLA. My daughter, calm thy fears; Messina's princess----
BEATRICE. Name her not again! At that ill-omened sound the chill of death Creeps through my trembling frame.

ISABELLA. My child! but hear me----

BEATRICE. She has two sons by mortal hate dissevered, Don Manuel and Don Caesar----

ISABELLA. 'Tis myself! Behold thy mother! BEATRICE. Have I heard thee? Speak!

ISABELLA. I am thy mother, and Messina's princess! BEATRICE. Art thou Don Manuel's and Don Caesar's mother? ISABELLA. And thine! They are thy brethren whom thou namest. BEATRICE. Oh, gleam of horrid light!

ISABELLA. What troubles thee? Say, whence this strange emotion?

BEATRICE. Yes! 'twas they! Now I remember all; no dream deceived me, They met--'tis fearful truth! Unhappy men! Where have ye hid him?

[She rushes towards the Chorus; they turn away from her. A funeral march is heard in the distance.

CHORUS. Horror! Horror!

ISABELLA. Hid! Speak--who is hid? and what is true? Ye stand In silent dull amaze--as though ye fathomed Her words of mystery! In your faltering tones-- Your brows--I read of horrors yet unknown, That would refrain my tongue! What is it? Tell me! I will know all! Why fix ye on the door That awe-struck gaze? What mournful music sounds? [The march is heard nearer.

Chorus (BOHEMUND). It comes! it comes! and all shall be declared With terrible voice. My mistress! steel thy heart, Be firm, and bear with courage what awaits thee-- For more than women's soul thy destined griefs Demand.

ISABELLA. What comes? and what awaits me? Hark With fearful tones the death-wail smites mine ear-- It echoes through the house! Where are my sons?

[The first Semi-chorus brings in the body of DON MANUEL on a bier, which is placed at the side of the stage. A black pall is spread over it.

ISABELLA, BEATRICE, DIEGO.

Both Choruses.

First Chorus (CAJETAN).

With sorrow in his train, From street to street the King of Terror glides; With stealthy foot, and slow, He creeps where'er the fleeting race Of man abides In turn at every gate Is heard the dreaded knock of fate, The message of unutterable woe!

BERENGAR.

When, in the sere And autumn leaves decayed, The mournful forest tells how quickly fade The glories of the year! When in the silent tomb oppressed, Frail man, with weight of days, Sinks to his tranquil rest; Contented nature but obeys Her everlasting law,-- The general doom awakes no shuddering awe! But, mortals, oh! prepare For mightier ills; with ruthless hand Fell murder cuts the holy band-- The kindred tie: insatiate death, With unrelenting rage, Bears to his bark the flower of blooming age!

CAJETAN. When clouds athwart the lowering sky Are driven-- when bursts with hollow moan The thunder's peal--our trembling bosoms own The might of awful destiny! Yet oft the lightning's glare Darts sudden through the cloudless air:-- Then in thy short delusive day Of bliss, oh! dread the treacherous snare; Nor prize the fleeting goods in vain, The flowers that bloom but to decay! Nor wealth, nor joy, nor aught but pain, Was e'er to mortal's lot secure:-- Our first best lesson--to endure!

ISABELLA. What shall I hear? What horrors lurk beneath This funeral pall?

[She steps towards the bier, but suddenly pauses, and stands irresolute.

Some strange, mysterious dread Enthrals my sense. I would approach, and sudden The ice-cold grasp of terror holds me back!

[To BEATRICE, who has thrown herself between her and the bier. Whate'er it be, I will unveil----

[On raising the pall she discovers the body of DON MANUEL. Eternal Powers! it is my son!

[She stands in mute horror. BEATRICE sinks to the ground with a shriek of anguish near the bier.

CHORUS. Unhappy mother! 'tis thy son. Thy lips Have uttered what my faltering tongue denied.

ISABELLA. My soul! My Manuel! Oh, eternal grief! And is it thus I see thee? Thus thy life Has bought thy sister from the spoiler's rage? Where was thy brother? Could no arm be found To shield thee? Oh, be cursed the hand that dug These gory wounds! A curse on her that bore The murderer of my son! Ten thousand curses On all their race!
CHORUS. Woe! Woe!

ISABELLA. And is it thus Ye keep your word, ye gods? Is this your truth? Alas for him that trusts with honest heart Your soothing wiles! Why have I hoped and trembled? And this the issue of my prayers! Attend, Ye terror-stricken witnesses, that feed Your gaze upon my anguish; learn to know How warning visions cheat, and boding seers But mock our credulous hopes; let none believe The voice of heaven! When in my teeming womb This daughter lay, her father, in a dream Saw from his nuptial couch two laurels grow, And in the midst a lily all in flames, That, catching swift the boughs and knotted stems Burst forth with crackling rage, and o'er the house Spread in one mighty sea of fire. Perplexed By this terrific dream my husband sought The counsels of the mystic art, and thus Pronounced the sage: "If I a daughter bore, The murderess of his sons, the destined spring Of ruin to our house, the baleful child Should see the light."

Chorus (CAJETAN and BOHEMUND). What hast thou said, my mistress? Woe! Woe!

ISABELLA. For this her ruthless father spoke The dire behest of death. I rescued her, The innocent, the doomed one; from my arms The babe was torn; to stay the curse of heaven, And save my sons, the mother gave her child; And now by robber hands her brother falls; My child is guiltless. Oh, she slew him not!

CHORUS. Woe! Woe!

ISABELLA. No trust the fabling readers of the stars Have e'er deserved. Hear how another spoke With comfort to my soul, and him I deemed Inspired to voice the secrets of the skies! "My daughter should unite in love the hearts Of my dissevered sons;" and thus their tales Of curse and blessing on her head proclaim Each other's falsehood. No, she ne'er has brought A curse, the innocent; nor time was given The blessed promise to fulfil; their tongues Were false alike; their boasted art is vain; With trick of words they cheat our credulous ears, Or are themselves deceived! Naught ye may know Of dark futurity, the sable streams Of hell the fountain of your hidden lore, Or yon bright spring of everlasting light! First Chorus (CAJETAN).

Woe! Woe! thy tongue refrain! Oh, pause, nor thus with impious rage The might of heaven profane; The holy oracles are wise-- Expect with awe thy coming destinies!

ISABELLA. My tongue shall speak as prompts my swelling heart; My griefs shall cry to heaven. Why do we lift Our suppliant hands, and at the sacred shrines Kneel to adore? Good, easy dupes! What win we From faith and pious awe? to touch with prayers The tenants of yon azure realms on high, Were hard as with an arrow's point to pierce The silvery moon. Hid is the womb of time, Impregnable to mortal glance, and deaf The adamantine walls of heaven rebound The voice of anguish:--Oh, 'tis one, whate'er The flight of birds--the aspect of the stars! The book of nature is a maze--a dream The sage's art--and every sign a falsehood!

Second Chorus (BOHEMUND).

Woe! Woe! Ill-fated woman, stay Thy maddening blasphemies; Thou but disown'st, with purblind eyes, The flaming orb of day! Confess the gods,--they dwell on high-- They circle thee with awful majesty! All the Knights.

Confess the gods--they dwell on high-- They circle thee with awful majesty!

BEATRICE. Why hast thou saved thy daughter, and defied The curse of heaven, that marked me in thy womb The child of woe? Short-sighted mother!--vain Thy little arts to cheat the doom declared By the all-wise interpreters, that knit The far and near; and, with prophetic ken, See the late harvest spring in times unborn. Oh, thou hast brought destruction on thy race, Withholding from the avenging gods their prey; Threefold, with new embittered rage, they ask The direful penalty; no thanks thy boon Of life deserves--the fatal gift was sorrow!

Second Chorus (BERENGAR) looking towards the door with signs of agitation.

Hark to the sound of dread! The rattling, brazen din I hear! Of hell-born snakes the hissing tones are near! Yes--'tis the furies' tread!

CAJETAN.

In crumbling ruin wide, Fall, fall, thou roof, and sink, thou trembling floor That bear'st the dread, unearthly stride! Ye sable damps arise! Mount from the abyss in smoky spray, And pall the brightness of the day! Vanish, ye guardian powers! They come! The avenging deities

DON CAESAR, ISABELLA, BEATRICE. The Chorus.

[On the entrance of DON CAESAR the Chorus station themselves before him imploringly. He remains standing alone in the centre of the stage.

BEATRICE. Alas! 'tis he----

ISABELLA (stepping to meet him). My Caesar! Oh, my son! And is it thus I meet the? Look! Behold! The crime of hand accursed!

[She leads him to the corpse.

First Chorus (CAJETAN, BERENGAR).

Break forth once more Ye wounds! Flow, flow, in swarthy flood, Thou streaming gore!

ISABELLA. Shuddering with earnest gaze, and motionless, Thou stand'st.--yes! there my hopes repose, and all That earth has of thy brother; in the bud Nipped is your concord's tender flower, nor ever With beauteous fruit shall glad a mother's eyes, DON CAESAR. Be comforted; thy sons, with honest heart, To peace aspired, but heaven's decree was blood!

ISABELLA. I know thou lovedst him well; I saw between ye, With joy, the bands old Nature sweetly twined; Thou wouldst have borne him in thy heart of hearts With rich atonement of long wasted years! But see--fell murder thwarts thy dear design, And naught remains but vengeance!

DON CAESAR. Come, my mother, This is no place for thee. Oh, haste and leave This sight of woe.

[He endeavors to drag her away.

ISABELLA (throwing herself into his arms). Thou livest! I have a son! BEATRICE. Alas! my mother!

DON CAESAR. On this faithful bosom Weep out thy pains; nor lost thy son,--his love Shall dwell immortal in thy Caesar's breast.

First Chorus (CAJETAN, BERENGAR, MANFRED).

Break forth, ye wounds! Dumb witness! the truth proclaim; Flow fast, thou gory stream!

ISABELLA (clasping the hands of DON CAESAR and BEATRICE). My children!

DON CAESAR. Oh, 'tis ecstasy! my mother, To see her in thy arms! henceforth in love A daughter--sister----

ISABELLA (interrupting him). Thou hast kept thy word. My son; to thee I owe the rescued one; Yes, thou hast sent her----

DON CAESAR (in astonishment). Whom, my mother, sayst thou, That I have sent? ISABELLA. She stands before thine eyes-- Thy sister. DON CAESAR. She! My sister?

ISABELLA. Ay, What other? DON CAESAR. My sister!

ISABELLA. Thou hast sent her to me! DON CAESAR. Horror! His sister, too! CHORUS. Woe! woe!

BEATRICE. Alas! my mother! ISABELLA. Speak! I am all amaze!

DON CASAR. Be cursed the day When I was born! ISABELLA. Eternal powers!

DON CAESAR. Accursed The womb that bore me; cursed the secret arts, The spring of all this woe; instant to crush thee, Though the dread thunder swept--ne'er should this arm Refrain the bolts of death: I slew my brother! Hear it and tremble! in her arms I found him; She was my love, my chosen bride; and he-- My brother--in her arms! Thou hast heard all! If it be true--oh, if she be my sister-- And his! then I have done a deed that mocks The power of sacrifice and prayers to ope The gates of mercy to my soul!

Chorus (BOHEMUND).

The tidings on thy heart dismayed Have burst, and naught remains; behold! 'Tis come, nor long delayed, Whate'er the warning seers foretold: They spoke the message from on high, Their lips proclaimed resistless destiny!

The mortal shall the curse fulfil Who seeks to turn predestined ill. ISABELLA. The gods have done their worst; if they be true Or false, 'tis one--for nothing they can add To this--the measure of their rage is full.

Why should I tremble that have naught to fear? My darling son lies murdered, and the living I call my son no more. Oh! I have borne And nourished at my breast a basilisk That stung my best-beloved child.

My daughter, haste, And leave this house of horrors--I devote it To the avenging fiends! In an evil hour 'Twas crime that brought me hither, and of crime The victim I depart. Unwillingly I came--in sorrow I have lived--despairing I quit these halls; on me, the innocent, Descends this weight of woe! Enough--'tis shown That Heaven is just, and oracles are true!

[Exit, followed by DIEGO.

BEATRICE, DON CAESAR, the Chorus.

DON CAESAR (detaining BEATRICE). My sister, wouldst thou leave me? On this head A mother's curse may fall--a brother's blood Cry with accusing voice to heaven--all nature Invoke eternal vengeance on my soul-- But thou--oh! curse me not--I cannot bear it!

[BEATRICE points with averted eyes to the body.

I have not slain thy lover! 'twas thy brother, And mine that fell beneath my sword; and near As the departed one, the living owns The ties of blood: remember, too, 'tis I That most a sister's pity need--for pure His spirit winged its flight, and I am guilty!

[BEATRICE bursts into an agony of tears.

Weep! I will blend my tears with thine--nay, more, I will avenge thy brother; but the lover-- Weep not for him--thy passionate, yearning tears My inmost heart. Oh! from the boundless depths Of our affliction, let me gather this, The last and only comfort--but to know That we are dear alike. One lot fulfilled Has made our rights and wretchedness the same; Entangled in one snare we fall together, Three hapless victims of unpitying fate, And share the mournful privilege of tears. But when I think that for the lover more Than for the brother bursts thy sorrow's tide, Then rage and envy mingle with my pain, And hope's last balm forsakes my withering soul? Nor joyful, as beseems, can I requite This inured shade:--yet after him content To mercy's throne my contrite spirit shall fly, Sped by this hand--if dying I may know That in one urn our ashes shall repose, With pious office of a sister's care.

[He throws his arms around her with passionate tenderness.

I loved thee, as I ne'er had loved before, When thou wert strange; and that I bear the curse Of brother's blood, 'tis but because I loved thee With measureless transport: love was all my guilt, But now thou art my sister, and I claim Soft pity's tribute.

[He regards her with inquiring glances, and an air of painful suspense--then turns away with vehemence.

No! in this dread presence I cannot bear these tears--my courage flies And doubt distracts my soul. Go, weep in secret-- Leave me in error's maze--but never, never, Behold me more: I will not look again On thee, nor on thy mother. Oh! how passion Laid bare her secret heart! She never loved me!

She mourned her best-loved son--that was her cry Of grief--and naught was mine but show of fondness! And thou art false as she! make no disguise--

Recoil with horror from my sight--this form Shall never shock thee more--begone forever!

[Exit.

[She stands irresolute in a tumult of conflicting passions--then tears herself from the spot.

Chorus (CAJETAN).

Happy the man--his lot I prize That far from pomps and turmoil vain, Childlike on nature's bosom lies Amid the stillness of the plain. My heart is sad in the princely hall, When from the towering pride of state, I see with headlong ruin fall, How swift! the good and great! And he--from fortune's storm at rest Smiles, in the quiet haven laid Who, timely warned, has owned how blest The refuge of the cloistered shade; To honor's race has bade farewell, Its idle joys and empty shows; Insatiate wishes learned to quell, And lulled in wisdom's calm repose:-- No more shall passion's maddening brood Impel the busy scenes to try, Nor on his peaceful cell intrude The form of sad humanity! 'Mid crowds and strife each mortal ill Abides'--the grisly train of woe Shuns like the pest the breezy hill, To haunt the smoky marts below.

BERENGAR, BOHEMUND, and MANFRED.

On the mountains is freedom! the breath of decay Never sullies the fresh flowing air; Oh, Nature is perfect wherever we stray; 'Tis man that deforms it with care.

The whole Chorus repeats.

On the mountains is freedom, etc., etc. DON CAESAR, the Chorus.

DON CAESAR (more collected). I use the princely rights--'tis the last time-- To give this body to the ground, and pay Fit honors to the dead. So mark, my friends, My bosom's firm resolve, and quick fulfil Your lord's behest. Fresh in your memory lives The mournful pomp, when to the tomb ye bore So late my royal sire; scarce in these halls Are stilled the echoes of the funeral wail; Another corpse succeeds, and in the grave Weighs down its fellow-dust--almost our torch With borrowed lustre from the last, may pierce The monumental gloom; and on the stair, Blends in one throng confused two mourning trains. Then in the sacred royal dome that guards

The ashes of my sire, prepare with speed The funeral rites; unseen of mortal eye, And noiseless be your task--let all be graced, As then, with circumstances of kingly state. BOHEMUND. My prince, it shall be quickly done; for still Upreared, the gorgeous catafalque recalls The dread solemnity; no hand disturbed The edifice of death.

DON CAESAR. The yawning grave Amid the haunts of life? No goodly sign Was this: the rites fulfilled, why lingered yet The trappings of the funeral show?

BOHEMUND. Your strife With fresh embittered hate o'er all Messina Woke discord's maddening flames, and from the deed Our cares withdrew--so resolute remained, And closed the sanctuary.

DON CAESAR. Make no delay; This very night fulfil your task, for well Beseems the midnight gloom! To-morrow's sun Shall find this palace cleansed of every stain, And light a happier race.

[Exit the Second Chorus, with the body of DON MANUEL.

CAJETAN. Shall I invite The brotherhood of monks, with rights ordained By holy church of old, to celebrate The office of departed souls, and hymn The buried one to everlasting rest?

DON CAESAR. Their strains above my tomb shall sound for ever Amid the torches' blaze--no solemn rites Beseem the day when gory murder scares Heaven's pardoning grace.

CAJETAN. Oh, let not wild despair Tempt thee to impious, rash resolve. My prince No mortal arm shall e'er avenge this deed; And penance calms, with soft, atoning power, The wrath on high.

DON CAESAR. If for eternal justice Earth has no minister, myself shall wield The avenging sword; though heaven, with gracious ear, Inclines to sinners' prayers, with blood alone Atoned is murder's guilt.

CAJETAN. To stem the tide Of dire misfortune, that with maddening rage Bursts o'er your house, were nobler than to pile Accumulated woe. DON CAESAR. The curse of old Shall die with me! Death self-imposed alone Can break the chain of fate.

CAJETAN. Thou owest thyself A sovereign to this orphaned land, by thee Robbed of its other lord!

DON CAESAR. The avenging gods Demand their prey--some other deity May guard the living!

CAJETAN. Wide as e'er the sun In glory beams, the realm of hope extends; But--oh remember! nothing may we gain From Death!

DON CAESAR. Remember thou thy vassal's duty; Remember and be silent! Leave to me To follow, as I list, the spirit of power That leads me to the goal. No happy one May look into my breast: but if thy prince Owns not a subject's homage, dread at least The murderer!--the accursed!--and to the head Of the unhappy--sacred to the gods-- Give honors due. The pangs that rend my soul-- What I have suffered--what I feel--have left No place for earthly thoughts!

DONNA ISABELLA, DON CAESAR, The Chorus.

ISABELLA (enters with hesitating steps, and looks irresolutely towards DON CAESAR; at last she approaches, and addresses him with collected tones). I thought mine eyes should ne'er behold thee more; Thus I had vowed despairing! Oh, my son! How quickly all a mother's strong resolves Melt into air! 'Twas but the cry of rage That stifled nature's pleading voice; but now What tidings of mysterious import call me From the desolate chambers of my sorrow? Shall I believe it? Is it true? one day Robs me of both my sons?

Chorus.

Behold! with willing steps and free, Thy son prepares to tread The paths of dark eternity The silent mansions of the dead. My prayers are vain; but thou, with power confessed, Of nature's holiest passion, storm his breast! ISABELLA. I call the curses back--that in the frenzy Of blind despair on thy beloved head I poured. A mother may not curse the child That from her nourishing breast drew life, and gave Sweet recompense for all her travail past; Heaven would not hear the impious vows; they fell With quick rebound, and heavy with my tears Down from the flaming vault! Live! live! my son! For I may rather bear to look on thee-- The murderer of one child--than weep for both!

DON CAESAR. Heedless and vain, my mother, are thy prayers For me and for thyself; I have no place Among the living: if thine eyes may brook The murderer's sight abhorred--I could not bear The mute reproach of thy eternal sorrow.

ISABELLA. Silent or loud, my son, reproach shall never Disturb thy breast--ne'er in these halls shall sound The voice of wailing, gently on my tears My griefs shall flow away: the sport alike Of pitiless fate together we will mourn, And veil the deed of blood.

DON CAESAR (with a faltering voice, and taking her hand). Thus it shall be, My mother--thus with silent, gentle woe Thy grief shall fade: but when one common tomb The murderer and his victim closes round-- When o'er our dust one monumental stone Is rolled--the curse shall cease--thy love no more Unequal bless thy sons: the precious tears Thine eyes of beauty weep shall sanctify Alike our memories. Yes! In death are quenched The fires of rage; and hatred owns subdued, The mighty reconciler. Pity bends An angel form above the funeral urn, With weeping, dear embrace. Then to the tomb Stay not my passage:--Oh, forbid me not, Thus with atoning sacrifice to quell The curse of heaven.

ISABELLA. All Christendom is rich In shrines of mercy, where the troubled heart May find repose. Oh! many a heavy burden Have sinners in Loretto's mansion laid; And Heaven's peculiar blessing breathes around The grave that has redeemed the world! The prayers Of the devout are precious--fraught with store Of grace, they win forgiveness from the skies;-- And on the soil by gory murder stained Shall rise the purifying fane. DON CAESAR. We pluck The arrow from the wound--but the torn heart Shall ne'er be healed. Let him who can, drag on A weary life of penance and of pain, To cleanse the spot of everlasting guilt;-- I would not live the victim of despair; No! I must meet with beaming eye the smile Of happy ones, and breathe erect the air Of liberty and joy. While yet alike We shared thy love, then o'er my days of youth Pale envy cast his withering shade; and now, Think'st thou my heart could brook the dearer ties That bind thee in thy sorrow to the dead? Death, in his undecaying palace throned, To the pure diamond of perfect virtue Sublimes the mortal, and with chastening fire Each gathered stain of frail humanity Purges and burns away: high as the stars Tower o'er this earthly sphere, he soars above me; And as by ancient hate dissevered long, Brethren and equal denizens we lived, So now my restless soul with envy pines, That he has won from me the glorious prize Of immortality, and like a god In memory marches on to times unborn!

ISABELLA. My Sons! Why have I called you to Messina To find for each a grave? I brought ye hither To calm your strife to peace. Lo! Fate has turned My hopes to blank despair.

DON CAESAR. Whate'er was spoke, My mother, is fulfilled! Blame not the end By Heaven ordained. We trode our father's halls With hopes of peace; and reconciled forever, Together we shall sleep in death.

ISABELLA. My son, Live for thy mother! In the stranger's land, Say, wouldst thou leave me friendless and alone, To cruel scorn a prey-- no filial arm To shield my helpless age?

DON CAESAR. When all the world With heartless taunts pursues thee, to our grave For refuge fly, my mother, and invoke Thy sons' divinity--we shall be gods! And we will hear thy prayers:--and as the twins Of heaven, a beaming star of comfort shine To the tossed shipman--we will hover near thee With present help, and soothe thy troubled soul!

ISABELLA. Live--for thy mother, live, my son-- Must I lose all? [She throws her arms about him with passionate emotion. He gently disengages himself, and turning his face away extends to her his hand.

DON CAESAR. Farewell!

ISABELLA. I can no more; Too well my tortured bosom owns how weak A mother's prayers: a mightier voice shall sound Resistless on thy heart.

[She goes towards the entrance of the scene.

My daughter, come. A brother calls him to the realms of night; Perchance with golden hues of earthly joy The sister, the beloved, may gently lure The wanderer to life again.

[BEATRICE appears at the entrance of the scene. DONNA ISABELLA, DON CAESAR, and the Chorus.

DON CAESAR (on seeing her, covers his face with his hands). My mother! What hast thou done?

ISABELLA (leading BEATRICE forwards). A mother's prayers are vain! Kneel at his feet--conjure him--melt his heart! Oh, bid him live!

DON CAESAR. Deceitful mother, thus Thou triest thy son! And wouldst thou stir my soul Again to passion's strife, and make the sun Beloved once more, now when I tread the paths Of everlasting night? See where he stands-- Angel of life!--and wondrous beautiful, Shakes from his plenteous horn the fragrant store Of golden fruits and flowers, that breathe around Divinest airs of joy;--my heart awakes In the warm sunbeam--hope returns, and life Thrills in my breast anew.

ISABELLA (to BEATRICE). Thou wilt prevail! Or none! Implore him that he live, nor rob The staff and comfort of our days. BEATRICE. The loved one A sacrifice demands. Oh, let me die To soothe a brother's shade! Yes, I will be The victim! Ere I saw the light forewarned To death, I live a wrong to heaven! The curse Pursues me still: 'twas I that slew thy son-- I waked the slumbering furies of their strife-- Be mine the atoning blood!

CAJETAN. Ill-fated mother! Impatient all thy children haste to doom, And leave thee on the desolate waste alone Of joyous life.

BEATRICE. Oh, spare thy precious days For nature's band. Thy mother needs a son; My brother, live for her! Light were the pang To lose a daughter--but a moment shown, Then snatched away!

DON CAESAR (with deep emotion). 'Tis one to live or die, Blest with a sister's love!

BEATRICE. Say, dost thou envy Thy brother's ashes?

DON CAESAR. In thy grief he lives A hallowed life!--my doom is death forever!

BEATRICE. My brother!

DON CAESAR. Sister! are thy tears for me? BEATRICE. Live for our mother!

DON CAESAR (dropping her hand, and stepping back). For our mother?

BEATRICE (hiding her head in his breast). Live For her and for thy sister! Chorus (BOHEMUND). She has won! Resistless are her prayers.

Despairing mother, Awake to hope again--his choice is made! Thy son shall live! [At this moment an anthem is heard. The folding doors are thrown open, and in the church is seen the catafalque erected, and the coffin surrounded with candlesticks.

DON CAESAR (turning to the coffin). I will not rob thee, brother! The sacrifice is thine:--Hark! from the tomb, Mightier than mother's tears, or sister's love, Thy voice resistless cries:--my arms enfold A treasure, potent with celestial joys, To deck this earthly sphere, and make a lot Worthy the gods! but shall I live in bliss, While in the tomb thy sainted innocence Sleeps unavenged? Thou, Ruler of our days, All just--all wise--let not the world behold Thy partial care! I saw her tears!--enough-- They flowed for me! I am content: my brother! I come!

[He stabs himself with a dagger, and falls dead at his sister's feet. She throws herself into her mother's arms.

Chorus, CAJETAN (after a deep silence). In dread amaze I stand, nor know If I should mourn his fate. One truth revealed Speaks in my breast;--no good supreme is life; But all of earthly ills the chief is--Guilt!

THE END

ON THE USE OF THE CHORUS IN TRAGEDY.

A poetical work must vindicate itself: if the execution be defective, little aid can be derived from commentaries.

On these grounds I might safely leave the chorus to be its own advocate, if we had ever seen it presented in an appropriate manner. But it must be remembered that a dramatic composition first assumes the character of a whole by means of representation on the stage. The poet supplies only the words, to which, in a lyrical tragedy, music and rhythmical motion are essential accessories. It follows, then, that if the chorus is deprived of accompaniments appealing so powerfully to the senses, it will appear a superfluity in the economy of the drama--a mere hinderance to the development of the plot--destructive to the illusion of the scene, and wearisome to the spectators.

To do justice to the chorus, more especially if our aims in poetry be of a grand and elevated character, we must transport ourselves from the actual to a possible stage. It is the privilege of art to furnish for itself whatever is requisite, and the accidental deficiency of auxiliaries ought not to confine the plastic imagination of the poet. He aspires to whatever is most dignified, he labors to realize the ideal in his own mind--though in the execution of his purpose he must needs accommodate himself to circumstances.

The assertion so commonly made that the public degrades art is not well founded. It is the artist that brings the public to the level of his own conceptions; and, in every age in which art has gone to decay, it has fallen through its professors. The people need feeling alone, and feeling they possess. They take their station before the curtain with an unvoiced longing, with a multifarious capacity. They bring with them an aptitude for what is highest--they derive the greatest pleasure from what is judicious and true; and if, with these powers of appreciation, they deign to be satisfied with inferior productions, still, if they have once tasted what is excellent, they will in the end insist on having it supplied to them.

It is sometimes objected that the poet may labor according to an ideal-- that the critic may judge from ideas, but that mere executive art is subject to contingencies, and depends for effect on the occasion. Managers will be obstinate; actors are bent on display--the audience is inattentive and unruly. Their object is relaxation, and they are disappointed if mental exertion be required, when they expected only amusement. But if the theatre be made instrumental towards higher objects, the diversion, of the spectator will not be increased, but ennobled. It will be a diversion, but a poetical one. All art is dedicated to pleasure, and there can be no higher and worthier end than to make men happy. The true art is that which provides the highest degree of pleasure; and this consists in the abandonment of the spirit to the free play of all its faculties. Every one expects from the imaginative arts a certain emancipation from the bounds of reality: we are willing to give a scope to fancy, and recreate ourselves with the possible. The man who expects it the least will nevertheless forget his ordinary pursuits, his everyday existence and individuality, and experience delight from uncommon incidents:--if he be of a serious turn of mind he will acknowledge on the stage that moral government of the world which he fails to discover in real life. But he is, at the same time, perfectly aware that all is an empty show, and that in a true sense he is feeding only on dreams. When he returns from the theatre to the world of realities, he is again compressed within its narrow bounds; he is its denizen as before--for it remains what it was, and in him nothing has been changed. What, then, has he gained beyond a momentary illusive pleasure which vanished with the occasion?

It is because a passing recreation is alone desired that a mere show of truth is thought sufficient. I mean that probability or vraisemblance which is so highly esteemed, but which the commonest workers are able to substitute for the true.

Art has for its object not merely to afford a transient pleasure, to excite to a momentary dream of liberty; its aim is to make us absolutely free; and this it accomplishes by awakening, exercising, and perfecting in us a power to remove to an objective distance the sensible world; (which otherwise only burdens us as rugged matter, and presses us down with a brute influence;) to transform it into the free working of our spirit, and thus acquire a dominion over the material by means of ideas. For the very reason also that true art requires somewhat of the objective and real, it is not satisfied with a show of truth. It rears its ideal edifice on truth itself--on the solid and deep foundations of nature.

But how art can be at once altogether ideal, yet in the strictest sense real; how it can entirely leave the actual, and yet harmonize with nature, is a problem to the multitude; and hence the distorted views which prevail in regard to poetical and plastic works; for to ordinary judgments these two requisites seem to counteract each other. It is commonly supposed that one may be attained by the sacrifice of the other;--the result is a failure to arrive at either. One to whom nature has given a true sensibility, but denied the plastic imaginative power, will be a faithful painter of the real; he will adapt casual appearances, but never catch the spirit of nature. He will only reproduce to us the matter of the world, which, not being our own work, the product of our creative spirit, can never have the beneficent operation of art, of which the essence is freedom. Serious indeed, but unpleasing, is the cast of thought with which such an artist and poet dismisses us; we feel ourselves painfully thrust back into the narrow sphere of reality by means of the very art which ought to have emancipated us. On the other hand, a writer endowed with a lively fancy, but destitute of warmth and individuality of feeling, will not concern himself in the least about truth; he will sport with the stuff of the world, and endeavor to surprise by whimsical combinations; and as his whole performance is nothing but foam and glitter, he will, it is true, engage the attention for a time, but build up and confirm nothing in the understanding. His playfulness is, like the gravity of the other, thoroughly unpoetical. To string together at will fantastical images is not to travel into the realm of the ideal; and the imitative reproduction of the actual cannot be called the representation of nature. Both requisites stand so little in contradiction to each other that they are rather one and the same thing; that art is only true insomuch as it altogether forsakes the actual, and becomes purely ideal.

Nature herself is an idea of the mind, and is never presented to the senses. She lies under the veil of appearances, but is herself never apparent. To the art of the ideal alone is lent, or rather absolutely given, the privilege to grasp the spirit of the all and bind it in a corporeal form.

Yet, in truth, even art cannot present it to the senses, but by means of her creative power to the imaginative faculty alone; and it is thus that she becomes more true than all reality, and more real than all experience. It follows from these premises that the artist can use no single element taken from reality as he finds it--that his work must be ideal in all its parts, if it be designed to have, as it were, an intrinsic reality, and to harmonize with nature. What is true of art and poetry, in the abstract, holds good as to their various kinds; and we may apply what has been advanced to the subject of tragedy. In this department it is still necessary to controvert the ordinary notion of the natural, with which poetry is altogether incompatible. A certain ideality has been allowed in painting, though, I fear, on grounds rather conventional than intrinsic; but in dramatic works what is desired is allusion, which, if it could be accomplished by means of the actual, would be, at best, a paltry deception. All the externals of a theatrical representation are opposed to this notion; all is merely a symbol of the real. The day itself in a theatre is an artificial one; the metrical dialogue is itself ideal; yet the conduct of the play must forsooth be real, and the general effect sacrificed to a part. Thus the French, who have utterly misconceived the spirit of the ancients, adopted on their stage the unities of tine and place in the most common and empirical sense; as though there were any place but the bare ideal one, or any other time than the mere sequence of the incidents.

By the introduction of a metrical dialogue an important progress has been made towards the poetical tragedy. A few lyrical dramas have been successful on the stage, and poetry, by its own living energy, has triumphed over prevailing prejudices. But so long as these erroneous views are entertained little has been done--for it is not enough barely to tolerate as a poetical license that which is, in truth, the essence of all poetry. The introduction of the chorus would be the last and decisive step; and if it only served this end, namely, to declare open and honorable warfare against naturalism in art, it would be for us a living wall which tragedy had drawn around herself, to guard her from contact with the world of reality, and maintain her own ideal soil, her poetical freedom.

It is well-known that the Greek tragedy had its origin in the chorus; and though in process of time it became independent, still it may be said that poetically, and in spirit, the chorus was the source of its existence, and that without these persevering supporters and witnesses of the incident a totally different order of poetry would have grown out of the drama. The abolition of the chorus, and the debasement of this sensibly powerful organ into the characterless substitute of a confidant, is by no means such an improvement in the tragedy as the French, and their imitators, would have it supposed to be.

The old tragedy, which at first only concerned itself with gods, heroes and kings introduced the chorus as an essential accompaniment. The poets found it in nature, and for that reason employed it. It grew out of the poetical aspect of real life. In the new tragedy it becomes an organ of art, which aids in making the poetry prominent. The modern poet no longer finds the chorus in nature; he must needs create and introduce it poetically; that is, he must resolve on such an adaption of his story as will admit of its retrocession to those primitive times and to that simple form of life.

The chorus thus renders more substantial service to the modern dramatist than to the old poet--and for this reason, that it transforms the commonplace actual world into the old poetical one; that it enables him to dispense with all that is repugnant to poetry, and conducts him back to the most simple, original, and genuine motives of action. The palaces of kings are in these days closed--courts of justice have been transferred from the gates of cities to the interior of buildings; writing has narrowed the province of speech; the people itself--the sensibly living mass--when it does not operate as brute force, has become a part of the civil polity, and thereby an abstract idea in our minds; the deities have returned within the bosoms of mankind. The poet must reopen the palaces--he must place courts of justice beneath the canopy of heaven--restore the gods, reproduce every extreme which the artificial frame of actual life has abolished--throw aside every factitious influence on the mind or condition of man which impedes the manifestation of his inward nature and primitive character, as the statuary rejects modern costume:--and of all external circumstances adopts nothing but what is palpable in the highest of forms--that of humanity.

But precisely as the painter throws around his figures draperies of ample volume, to fill up the space of his picture richly and gracefully, to arrange its several parts in harmonious masses, to give due play to color, which charms and refreshes the eye--and at once to envelop human forms in a spiritual veil, and make them visible--so the tragic poet inlays and entwines his rigidly contracted plot and the strong outlines of his characters with a tissue of lyrical magnificence, in which, as in flowing robes of purple, they move freely and nobly, with a sustained dignity and exalted repose.

In a higher organization, the material, or the elementary, need not be visible; the chemical color vanishes in the finer tints of the imaginative one. The material, however, has its peculiar effect, and may be included in an artistical composition. But it must deserve its place by animation, fulness and harmony, and give value to the ideal forms which it surrounds instead of stifling them by its weight.

In respect of the pictorial art, this is obvious to ordinary apprehension, yet in poetry likewise, and in the tragical kind, which is our immediate subject, the same doctrine holds good. Whatever fascinates the senses alone is mere matter, and the rude element of a work of art:-- if it takes the lead it will inevitably destroy the poetical--which lies at the exact medium between the ideal and the sensible. But man is so constituted that he is ever impatient to pass from what is fanciful to what is common; and reflection must, therefore, have its place even in tragedy. But to merit this place it must, by means of delivery, recover what it wants in actual life; for if the two elements of poetry, the ideal and the sensible, do not operate with an inward mutuality, they must at least act as allies--or poetry is out of the question. If the balance be not intrinsically perfect, the equipoise can only be maintained by an agitation of both scales.

This is what the chorus effects in tragedy. It is in itself, not an individual but a general conception; yet it is represented by a palpable body which appeals to the senses with an imposing grandeur. It forsakes the contracted sphere of the incidents to dilate itself over the past and the future, over distant times and nations, and general humanity, to deduce the grand results of life, and pronounce the lessons of wisdom. But all this it does with the full power of fancy--with a bold lyrical freedom which ascends, as with godlike step, to the topmost height of worldly things; and it effects it in conjunction with the whole sensible influence of melody and rhythm, in tones and movements. The chorus thus exercises a purifying influence on tragic poetry, insomuch as it keeps reflection apart from the incidents, and by this separation arms it with a poetical vigor, as the painter, by means of a rich drapery, changes the ordinary poverty of costume into a charm and ornament.

But as the painter finds himself obliged to strengthen the tone of color of the living subject, in order to counterbalance the material influences--so the lyrical effusions of the chorus impose upon the poet the necessity of a proportionate elevation of his general diction. It is the chorus alone which entitles the poet to employ this fulness of tone, which at once charms the senses, pervades the spirit, and expands the mind. This one giant form on his canvas obliges him to mount all his figures on the cothurnus, and thus impart a tragical grandeur to his picture. If the chorus be taken away, the diction of the tragedy must generally be lowered, or what is now great and majestic will appear forced and overstrained. The old chorus introduced into the French tragedy would present it in all its poverty, and reduce it to nothing; yet, without doubt, the same accompaniment would impart to Shakspeare's tragedy its true significance.

As the chorus gives life to the language--so also it gives repose to the action; but it is that beautiful and lofty repose which is the characteristic of a true work of art. For the mind of the spectator ought to maintain its freedom through the most impassioned scenes; it should not be the mere prey of impressions, but calmly and severely detach itself from the emotions which it suffers. The commonplace objection made to the chorus, that it disturbs the illusion, and blunts the edge of the feelings, is what constitutes its highest recommendation; for it is this blind force of the affections which the true artist deprecates--this illusion is what he disdains to excite. If the strokes which tragedy inflicts on our bosoms followed without respite, the passion would overpower the action. We should mix ourselves with the subject-matter, and no longer stand above it. It is by holding asunder the different parts, and stepping between the passions with its composing views, that the chorus restores to us our freedom, which would else be lost in the tempest. The characters of the drama need this intermission in order to collect themselves; for they are no real beings who obey the impulse of the moment, and merely represent individuals--but ideal persons and representatives of their species, who enunciate the deep things of humanity.

Thus much on my attempt to revive the old chorus on the tragic stage. It is true that choruses are not unknown to modern tragedy; but the chorus of the Greek drama, as I have employed it--the chorus, as a single ideal person, furthering and accompanying the whole plot--if of an entirely distinct character; and when, in discussion on the Greek tragedy, I hear mention made of choruses, I generally suspect the speaker's ignorance of his subject. In my view the chorus has never been reproduced since the decline of the old tragedy.

I have divided it into two parts, and represented it in contest with itself; but this occurs where it acts as a real person, and as an unthinking multitude.

As chorus and an ideal person it is always one and entire. I have also several times dispensed with its presence on the stage. For this liberty I have the example of Aeschylus, the creator of tragedy, and Sophocles, the greatest master of his art.

Another license it may be more difficult to excuse. I have blended together the Christian religion and the pagan mythology, and introduced recollections of the Moorish superstition. But the scene of the drama is Messina--where these three religions either exercised a living influence, or appealed to the senses in monumental remains. Besides, I consider it a privilege of poetry to deal with different religions as a collective whole. In which everything that bears an individual character, and expresses a peculiar mode of feeling, has its place. Religion itself, the idea of a Divine Power, lies under the veil of all religions; and it must be permitted to the poet to represent it in the form which appears the most appropriate to his subject.

Made in the USA
Columbia, SC
24 November 2023